SUSTAINING OUR SPIRITS:

WOMEN LEADERS THRIVING FOR TODAY AND TOMORROW

D1538098

NASW PRESS

National Association of Social Workers
Washington, DC

Elvira Craig de Silva, DSW, *President*
Elizabeth J. Clark, PhD, ACSW, MPH, *Executive Director*

Darlyne
Bailey

Kelly
McNally Koney

Mary Ellen
McNish

Ruthmary
Powers

and

Katrina
Uhly

Cheryl Y. Bradley, *Publisher*
Marcia Roman, *Managing Editor*
Lisa M. O'Hearn, *Project Manager and Staff Editor*
Mary Killion, *Copyeditor*
Cara Schumacher, *Proofreader*
Bernice Eisen, *Indexer*

Cover by Eye to Eye Designs
Interior design by Circle Graphics
Printed and bound by Victor Graphics

Library of Congress Cataloging-in-Publication Data

Sustaining our spirits: women leaders thriving for today and tomorrow /
Darlyne Bailey. . .[et al.]
p. cm.
Includes bibliographical references.
ISBN 978-0-87101-382-8
1. Leadership in women. 2. Spiritual life. 3. Women—Conduct of life. 4. Feminism. I. Bailey,
Darlyne, 1952–
HQ1233.S87 2008
158'.4082–dc22

Printed in the United States of America

Dedication

The book that you're holding in your hands is dedicated to all women—past, present, and future—who are committed to using their leadership talents and responsibilities for the good.

This includes Iris Bailey, Sharon Robinson, Winnie Burch, Dawn and Tara, Jean, Ella, and the Bolden-Ledford family (Darlyne Bailey); all the amazing and inspiring women in my family and my life—you help sustain me always (Kelly McNally Koney); Glenna McNish Harkins and all young women leaders who will change the world (Mary Ellen McNish); Laura and Lauren, Kristen, Jackie and Julia, and Kelly (Ruthmary Powers); Katharine B., Katie E., Paola P., Cathy U., and Renée W. (Katrina Uhly).

To all, we simply say thank you.

Contents

Foreword   vii
Frances Hesselbein

Prologue   ix
Darlyne Bailey

PART ONE

1   Contexts and Core Concepts, Processes, and Products   1

2   Spiritual Leadership for Our Organizations of the Future   17

3   Leading Through the Earthview   29

PART TWO

4   Organizational Toxicity and Toxin Handlers   41

5   Self-Knowledge as a Foundation for Sustenance   59

6   Aligning Our Mission   67

7   Personal and Organizational Balance and Boundaries   79

8   Dis-Covering Community   87

9   Connecting the Present and the Future through
Role Models and Mentoring   95

10   A Habitat for Sustainability—Coming Home   103

Epilogue: From Evolutionary to Revolutionary Leadership—
Leading Into the Future   109

Acknowledgments—Thank You!   113

Appendix   115

Works Cited   117

Bibliography   123

Foreword

Sustaining Our Spirits provides an authentic, real-life experience, rooted in research, with perspectives rarely examined in depth. This is a handbook for life's journey for leaders who are women.

The significance of this new book can be celebrated by women everywhere, as they test, absorb, and make the lessons learned their own. This resource is not about theory but about lives fully lived and examined by eminently successful leaders—the great days, the tough days, the lessons applied and generously shared.

I found support for my view, a variation of Peter Drucker's advice to concentrate on the tasks, rather than the gender. We are not a category. We are leaders who are women, and we are in the leadership positions we hold because of what we bring to the job, not because of our gender. Yet, you and I know our gender adds a very special dimension to our work and to the positions we hold.

And therein lies the delicate balance. We need to see ourselves life-size in these positions, these organizations, these communities and to help others see us life-size in our contributions, our examples—not through "I am woman," but through our presence, our performance, our results. At the same time, we need to appreciate that one of our leadership imperatives is to recognize the context, the backdrop of our times, against which we measure the present opportunities and the doors that are open to women who lead at every level, even as we recognize those barriers that still exist. These barriers provide an opportunity for us to take the lead, find the partners, forge the alliances and collaborations to open doors, and bring new understanding of the power of the richly diverse, richly inclusive enterprise. As women who can lead at every level and with the significance our society requires and deserves, we ask ourselves, "Beyond my present leadership position, am I communicating the values, the quality, the generous spirit—am I helping others and building the leaders of the future for the organization of the future?"

Here is where the spirit within, the leader within, move us beyond where we are to where we are called to be. When we listen to the whispers of our lives (and something in our genes gives us the ability to listen to that quiet voice within), we rise and move far beyond the old expectations.

It has never been more difficult for girls and young women growing up in the world. There are massive negative forces against their healthy growing up; yet, in our age, as these remarkable authors in this book communicate in word and example, new opportunities are far greater than the obstacles when women help, support, serve as role models, and mentor other women, communicating the remarkable possibilities that lie ahead. So, we discard old preconceptions of gender barriers, recognize those that do still exist, and pour our energy into building and sustaining an inclusive, diverse enterprise that provides rich and equal access to all of its people.

We recognize the remarkable spirits, examples, caring, and sharing of the leaders who have written this journey *for* the journey; all of them demonstrating that leadership is a journey—not a destination. We take their example, make it our own, and marvel at their present success as women of spirit and leaders of significance and achievement who know they are called to shine a light in the darkness of our times.

When we recognize the power of values lived, of our goals defined, of helping others along the way, we illuminate the lives of others, the spirit within; life shines ever more brightly, and all of it is circular and connected.

When we quietly think back upon all of the people, men and women, who encouraged us, helped us along the way, we realize that it was often not an action but the spirit within that communicated faith, courage, strength—an appreciation of who we are as women, as leaders, and who we could be. Called to lead, called to serve, called to change lives.

When we change lives, we find that we, ourselves, our own lives, are changed as women, as leaders, and as fellow travelers on the journey to significance, "sustaining our spirits."

Frances Hesselbein
Founding President and Chairman of the Leader to Leader Institute
(Formerly the Peter F. Drucker Foundation for Nonprofit Management)
Former CEO, Girl Scouts of the USA
New York, NY

Prologue

*Don't worry, Darlyne. A leader does not have to have
all of the answers. Rather, a good leader has to make
sure that all the right questions are on the table.*

—Paulo Freire, personal communication, 1994

Do women absorb the toxicity of an organization to help sustain it? If so, how do
they thrive and even survive as individuals and as leaders? What rituals, practices, knowledge, and strategies have they found to manage the paradoxes inherent in
leading fully while living fully?

Women's leadership has been an area of popular interest and academic study for
the past several decades. Publications have focused on the responsibilities and roles of
women in leadership, the ways in which they work and lead, and their similarities and
differences in comparison to their male counterparts. Despite this public attention and
the corresponding rise in the number of women in formal leadership positions, women
leaders can be likened to an endangered species. Women who lead are not unlike the
many animals and plants around the world that face real peril when they lack a consistent, nurturing habitat to ensure their sustainability. The *Sustaining Our Spirits* project
was conceived as an opportunity to discover and disseminate strategies for securing the
viability of our women leaders now and into the future.

Recognition of the need for this work came from experiences within my career
journey—more than 20 years as an administrator, initially in nonprofit organizations
and then in academia—and in manifold conversations with colleagues. It was through
these encounters that two truths became apparent. First, despite the increasing number
of resources available, strong, compassionate, and effective leadership was hard, not
only for women, but for everyone. And second, the paths of women, regardless of
whether they worked in corporate, government, faith-based, or other social sector
settings, seemed to contain many more bumps, potholes, and even land mines than
those of their male counterparts. The growing successes of women as organizational,

community, and political leaders had not diminished this reality. As women and as leaders, we seemed to search for safe places in which to connect with each other, give voice to our stories, and re-energize our souls for our benefit and the benefit of those who shared our journeys.

For me, becoming a newly minted Group XIII member of the W.K. Kellogg National Fellowship Program served as the catalyst for an unanticipated sojourn to São Paulo, Brazil, to meet and learn from the educator-activist, Paulo Freire. Emboldened by my acceptance into this incredible leadership program, I telephoned Dr. Freire one afternoon, and he invited me to his home for a visit. This 10-day exchange of honest questions, concerns, and ideas in community with Dr. Freire, some of my Fellows, and one of our advisors resulted in a deepened conviction about the power of relationship through dialogue to produce individual- and group-level change and growth. The core of my leadership style and work in building and discovering organizational and boundary-spanning communities will forever carry the imprint of this experience—this treasured time with a man with whom I was honored thereafter to spend more time and, ultimately, call my friend.

From Freire, I learned that time and space are essential to fostering authentic relationships and facilitating the work of any collective. Over the years, I thought about and then one day deliberately sought to co-create a project where women leaders would learn from and with one another how to sustain our life energies and commitment and, in turn, be able to share those lessons with others. Thus was born the *Sustaining Our Spirits* project.

Through *Sustaining Our Spirits,* we used the attribute of relationship building to design a process for a group of nine women leaders from across the United States. The intention was to provide the necessary space and time to individually share our leadership stories and collectively identify, develop, and document strategies that actually worked to sustain us, professionally and personally.

We began by meeting together in a series of four-day retreats over the course of a year. For a number of us, this work then evolved into much more over the following three years. One of the coauthors of this book describes her desire to participate this way:

> As a CEO of an international organization, I try to set the example that taking time to go to that deep place to stay centered is an important ingredient for success. With such a busy schedule, it is the hardest thing for me to do. I have been serving in this position for a little over two years. While I have strong allies on the board and within the staff, I often find myself wishing for deeper connections with other women leaders from outside the organization who would understand and empathize with some of my challenges. Our retreats provide that and so much more for me. They are a well I can dip into . . . without them are many more dry times.

Very soon, we began to see that stories like these were shared and were more common than we realized. For that reason, *Sustaining Our Spirits* became our approach to developing the capacity of women leaders to thrive. The process sought to respond to the fundamental needs of women in leadership through ongoing dialogue; bringing together women who were actively living leadership, as one of our heroes, Frances Hesselbein (2002), depicts it, as a matter of "how to be, not how to do it" (p. 3).

Sustaining Our Spirits reached out to women who were making significant contributions to their institutions, organizations, and communities. In providing them space for deep personal reflection and discovery, peer mentorship, and mutual support, we created lasting friendships and networks.

After each retreat concluded and we left our physical circle, we carried our individual and collective strengths with us into the broader world. As we talked about the project with others, it became clear that many more wanted to join us. Our journeys mirrored their journeys. Excited by the prospect of engaging other women in this transformative work, we began enlisting their participation through conversations and focused interviews. The results were affirming, exhilarating, and humbling.

We have been fortunate. We have had the chance to tell our stories and listen to the stories of others. We have all been positively impacted by this work and the wisdom generated by our ever-growing circle of women. We paid close attention and documented all that we heard—the joys, struggles, strategies, and dreams for the future that emerged through our retreats and our conversations with others. This book is an attempt to share these interactions. We do so not simply because we believe that what we learned is important but because, over and over, the women we met and spoke with about this work told us that sharing our lessons is essential. So now it is our honor and responsibility to broaden the circle, connecting with women and men like you who are committed to discovering how women can sustain themselves and begin to thrive as leaders.

My coauthors and I join in believing that *Sustaining Our Spirits* can make a difference for many over the years to come. If, today, women leaders are an endangered species, by collectively exploring those elements of our world that most challenge us and nurturing those that most enable us to flourish, we can learn how to manage what threatens us and strengthen the healthy sustainability of ourselves and our organizations. We believe that there are few better ways to serve the world.

Thank you for expanding our circle by joining us on this journey.

With best regards,

Darlyne

PART ONE

CHAPTER ONE

Contexts and Core Concepts, Processes, and Products

*When we do the best that we can, we never know what
miracle is wrought in our life, or in the life of another.*

—Attributed to Helen Keller

Beginning the Circle

The *Sustaining Our Spirits* initiative emerged from the dream of one woman. It was based in over two decades of experience leading in the nonprofit and academic worlds where she was often the first African American and usually the first woman in her leadership positions. The combination of her experiences and numerous conversations with other female colleagues who reported sharing many of the same struggles and desires provided the final impetus to do something different, something that would build on the life-giving forces of women in leadership. Listening to her own dreams and desires as well as those of her friends and colleagues, she ventured to create a space for women leaders to come together to discuss their joys and challenges and explore what is needed to keep their souls strong in the highly rewarding, often strenuous—sometimes even dangerous—world of leadership.

> *Dream big and make plans big enough to hold those dreams. Don't feel constrained by the local context we're in.*
>
> (Interviewee)

Interconnectivity

Innately appreciating and understanding the interconnectivity of life, in the face of the growing individualism of our culture, the founding leader of *Sustaining Our Spirits* brought together other women leaders from the nonprofit, faith-based, public, and for-profit arenas to explore the nature of relationships. She dreamed of delving more deeply into those forces that help leaders transcend the everyday chaos and thrive not only in the workplace but in all aspects of life. To begin this vital journey, she reached out to women in various leadership roles and disciplines, who, in turn, reached out to and were joined by others using what researchers refer to as a *networking* or a *snowball sampling,* wherein existing study participants recruit other participants from among people they know, therefore growing the sample like a rolling snowball. Those of us who came together in the initial retreats shared our service as leaders of communities and organizations. Even though we were all women leading in some capacity, we were all different. Spanning multiple educational and socioeconomic histories with differing identities in terms of age, race and ethnicity, religion, political perspectives, and sexual orientation, ours was a collective that included diversity in its voices. We were all women with an overwhelming desire to find support for our own leadership in the company of a caring and compassionate community, and we all had the daring to reveal our own experiences with the hope of benefiting others.

> Once you are identified as a leader, you sort of carry yourself like that, and people naturally know that you're the person they can go to, and trust to lead them, and help them to figure out what they're trying to do.
>
> **(Interviewee)**

Together we acknowledged that to be most meaningful, many of our interactions would need to transcend the realms in which we were most used to operating. We needed to create a safe place in which to engage in deep reflection and authentic dialogue. As we will discuss throughout this book, within our circle we learned that these practices were essential to the self-care we required. To do this we had to go beyond (and sometimes beneath) the physical, mental, and emotional levels at which we were most accustomed and felt most comfortable. If we were to truly cherish our connections, our work needed to embody and emanate from our fundamental essence— our souls, our spirits. We increasingly realized that when we embraced our own spirits, we shared even deeper connections with others. When we ignored or were blocked from nurturing our deepest selves, we were unable to fully see our interconnections. It was during those times that we found ourselves out of balance and quite frequently feeling unhealthy. A core of interrelatedness was what we found we most needed to nurture if we were to fortify ourselves and contribute to broader personal, organizational, community, and, ultimately, global healing.

> The definition of a leader that I use is one who is able to mobilize people and resources toward the common good. . . . It's a catalytic role that brings people and stuff— institutions—together to focus on something that is in the common good and to mobilize the collective action to make that happen.
>
> **(Interviewee)**

Using Retreats to Go Inside and Out

Sustaining Our Spirits began with a series of four retreats spread throughout the first year, followed by three years of further exploration. Every three months we gathered around the exploration of three essential questions: What sustains us as leaders? What threatens or challenges our sustainability? What wisdom do we want to pass on to the women coming after us? During the retreats, we created various opportunities and utilized multiple modalities to explore connections within ourselves, with each other, and with the world. We incorporated time for dialogue, reflection, rituals, and facilitated experiences to examine the challenges that we face as leaders in an increasingly turbulent world. From these purposeful encounters of communal sharing, we began to gather learnings that we felt needed to be passed along to the women leaders to come. Little did we know there would be so many who wanted to be heard.

As is true throughout life, our journey as a group of strong women leaders took a number of turns that we could neither predict nor control. We grew together and we fell apart and grew together again, individually and as a collective. Like the heroes and heroines of many great epics who embarked on their journeys with a single destination in mind only to discover that their expectations and assumptions were challenged and changed as the adventure unfolded, our explorations in retreat produced a richness of learning that far surpassed our original expectations.

As one of our participants so clearly stated from the outset, we wanted to "use our power for good." We anticipated that by mobilizing our communal energy with positive intention we might reap immediate and enduring benefits ourselves. We hoped that by chronicling and disseminating our collective wisdom, we could similarly help others. As we continued to reach deeper for answers to our three central questions, our discoveries germinated; they took root and blossomed into new insights about leadership and spirituality for oneself and for others. As we have moved forward, the cultivation of the seedlings in this process has become, for some of us, a life's vocation.

> *Sometimes I just want to talk to people who just know where I am coming from.*
>
> (Interviewee)

> *I find that in order to be sustained, my biggest struggle, and for other women leaders I know, is to feed ourselves. The first place you have to feed is your spiritual self . . . to believe that it is important. There is a reason that when you're on the airplane and they demonstrate what to do if there is an accident, they tell you to put on your own air mask before you attend to someone else. You have to be strong, and you have to be around. Every human being deserves the chance to make him/herself happy and joyful.*
>
> (Interviewee)

FIVE TOUCHSTONES OF OUR RETREATS

We originally envisaged our experience together to consist of focused, facilitated retreats, which would serve as the primary forum for analyzing and synthesizing our learning. The venues for this work highlighted our recognition of the relationships that exist between ourselves and our environments. Our retreat locations, therefore, were important and purposefully selected. The concepts of *reflection, dialogue, metaphor, paradox,* and *ritual* were core to our times together as they forced us to focus on one another and within ourselves. We found that these five concepts also solidified our connection with our planet, its rhythms, and its processes, and drove the content of our work together.

Reflection

We arranged the first four retreats to take place in serene, natural settings to accentuate human interdependence with Earth. Celebrating what was around us, the world we shared, we collectively and individually reflected upon our lives. These opportunities refreshed and invigorated us. They helped us to connect with each other as well as to establish a personal center for mindfulness—being fully awake, present—that more strongly linked us with something vast and ongoing, something greater than ourselves. During our daily experiences, by both observing and participating with our surrounding environment, we were reminded of our interconnections. We took time to journal and to record the many lessons that we learned. On a walk one afternoon, for example, a group of us came upon a spiderweb that stretched several feet between two trees. It was beautiful, and it forced us to pause in wonder. One of our participants recounted the experience this way:

> Our group almost literally ran into a big spiderweb during our reflection time this afternoon. I had been talking about this the day before, watching a spider in its web blow in the wind . . . We talked about what it might mean for us, right then—flexibility, strength, being centered. Even though it doesn't look strong, the spider carries the web with her wherever she goes. She is at home in herself. She can set up a web wherever she is. It is gorgeous. With it she can catch food, which is necessary for her survival. If someone walks through it, the web sticks to the person but it doesn't destroy her; she simply starts again and builds a new one.

The spider is adaptable; she survives and may even thrive in the face of predators, natural disasters, and human interference. Fundamentally, isn't that a way of being for which we all strive? Certainly, that was true for those of us involved in *Sustaining Our Spirits,* and we continued to hear that message from other women, too.

In addition to connecting us with the larger world, our retreats provided a safe and sacred place to rest and renew vital energy. The immediate benefits affected us so profoundly that one of us actually postponed back surgery to attend a retreat because she knew how valuable these communal experiences were for her:

> I, too, am grateful to be here. I postponed surgery and people thought I was nuts, but that's how important it is to be back. What happened [at our last retreat], I had forgotten. The uproariously funny conversations! I had lost all that between then and now. I am happy to be back. I am open to the possibilities.

Dialogue

Genuine dialogue was another foundational component in our retreat experience. As best defined by Paulo Freire (1981), the Brazilian educator who was once exiled from his country for teaching the poor how to read, dialogue is an "act of creation" (p. 77). Dialogue is a process in which two or more people discuss a topic by sharing opinions and simultaneously being open to the opinions of the other(s). It involves positive regard (for self and other), trust (in self and other), and unconditional caring (of self and other) (Freire, 1981). Unlike many of our personal exchanges and workplace discussions and meetings, dialogue is not simply a conversation where one person talks and the other listens, and it is definitely not where everyone talks and no one listens! It is less about convincing someone of something or proving a point. It is about listening, inquiring, and creating mutual understanding.

Although honest dialogue is not the default mode of interaction in most groups today, it can be. Imagine the benefits to our organizations and communities. Think about a time when you talked with someone and you felt really understood, a time when you experienced that person genuinely hearing you. How did you feel? What did the other person do or say that helped you know you were being heard? What changes did this realization mean for you? How did you respond? What was the outcome? Most likely you felt more comfortable to open up and listen to her or him. It's contagious. Often as leaders, we feel the need to control conversations to reach a desired outcome or the people with whom we are conversing feel they need to do so with us. True dialogue overcomes this tendency through an open-hearted and open-minded exchange of thoughts and feelings—an opening up and honoring of one another that, as Freire taught, can only come from the integration of humility, faith, hope, and love.

As we describe later, humility is a central component for leaders who are able to connect within themselves and beyond to others. When we are grounded, we are secure enough to appreciate our individuality and the value of each person within the whole. True humility allows us to take in the ideas and feelings of others and to understand and use criticism wisely.

The second component of dialogue is faith. Faith is about "understanding that living with uncertainty is okay; it is about walking forward and knowing that the ground will meet your feet" (Bailey, 2006, p. 300). Faith runs counter to fear; even though fear will always be present, as leaders, we must not be beholden to it. When we have faith, we are able to put aside our preconceived notions for the results of our interactions. If we approach dialogue in good faith and with faith, we can trust that the outcome will be beneficial and will be made more so by the richness of creativity that can come from people working from a place of mutual understanding.

Also essential to dialogue is hope. Hope is a belief in the reality that more and better can and will come for us all. It begins our search for wholeness—a search that can only be carried out when we work together with others. Hope is what kept alive all those who came before us; it is the wind in the sails of faith. It is what gets us up every morning; it is why we take care of ourselves and our relationships. When we are hopeful, optimism grows and dreams soar to create environments of possibility within ourselves, our workplaces, and in the rest of our lives.

Finally, at the very heart of dialogue is love. This is the incredibly special type of love, referred to as *agape*. As we will describe more fully, agape is a love for all simply because they exist, "not because of who they are, what they have done, or whom or what they know" (Bailey, 2006, p. 302). As leaders, this type of love fuels our compassion and patience to engage with others equally, which only serves to heighten the potential for dialogue.

Together, humility, faith, hope, and love form the foundation of dialogue and our ability to discover and create communities that are inclusive and safe. These spaces draw in people, further enhancing their lives inside and outside of their places of work. We know that people who work in organizations that value collectivity and community report greater career satisfaction and organizational commitment than those that prize individualism (Jandeska & Kraimer, 2005, p. 470). As we found in our reflections and experiences—our stories—dialogue with one another is an effective way to capture creative ideas that, however partial or fleeting, may become the source of new life and energy for the future. Such open-hearted and open-minded exchanges also lay the foundation for communities of trust, invoking a sense of responsibility to one another, which builds ethical, caring decision making. Leaders in real situations need the integration of everyone's talents to assist them in making thoughtful and clear decisions that do not have (unintended) consequences hurtful to others, their organizations, or themselves.

Metaphor

Metaphor was also elemental in our retreats. Yet, what is a metaphor for? Metaphor has been conceptualized as a way to bring a personal sense of "aliveness" to life and work (Leider, 2004); however, it is also an especially useful way to conceptualize community and relationships in our daily lives. In his book, *A Whole New Mind,* author and former White House speechwriter Daniel Pink (2005) defines metaphor as "understanding one thing in terms of something else . . . a whole-minded ability that some cognitive scientists have called 'imaginative rationality'" (p. 139). Although not many of us have been schooled in the construction of powerful metaphors (and we may have even at times arrived at what Howard Gardner, 2006, calls "felicitous metaphors"), this ability to interpret and share the world through multiple lenses resonated with us as we explored the many aspects of human relationships in our workplaces, especially as we attempted to describe our experiences of community.

> *I always looked at my role as a Dean as—I wouldn't necessarily use the word 'ministry'—that sounds a little too self-serving . . . but I always felt that I had a flock—a community of people for whom I was responsible—all the faculty, the students, the staff. . . . So, I had to think about all of those people as part of my flock that I had to look after. I felt this responsibility to do right by the people who were in my organization.*
>
> **(Interviewee)**

Paradox

A holistic, interconnected view of life suggests that leadership contains more ambiguity than certainty. In fact, it might be considered paradoxical. Paradox presents a both/and way of being, a circular perspective. Because there is often no single right or wrong answer or no clear path, inherent and fundamental tensions exist in managing paradox. Living with paradox is not necessarily comfortable, although acknowledging and understanding the realities of paradox can help us manage the inherent challenges of life and birth new systems and processes (Handy, 1994). Indeed, paradox is central in many major world philosophies and religions, from Shiva's dance as creator and destroyer to the Tao's yin and yang, to the Judeo-

Christian's creation story of shadow and light and peace and chaos, to much of the Sufi teachings through riddles and stories. In their most affirming way, paradoxes can be likened to pseudoquestions or riddles that "suspend us between too many good answers" (Sorensen, 2005, p. xii). As leaders we can facilitate the emergence of the most appropriate choices, confident in the fact that there will be many more opportunities to choose again.

Nonetheless, the pressures of facing paradoxes day-in and day-out can be daunting. Whether we consciously recognized them or not, paradoxes were the forces that ultimately led each of us to participate in the *Sustaining Our Spirits* project. Our isolation as leaders encouraged us to search out and offer to others a community of safe space and time free from contradictions between our espoused values and enacted behaviors—a consistent gathering in which we could tell our stories and connect and grow in our leadership roles. Yet, at the same time that many of us felt (and continue to believe) that we, as women leaders, are in danger—an endangered species living in a hostile world—we also knew that we had the potential to help shape the future for ourselves and for the next generations.

Throughout the entire *Sustaining Our Spirits* journey, we have reflected on and engaged in dialogue about the paradoxes of leadership and our roles within it. We focused on ourselves, on each other, on the women that came before us, and on those who will come after, and we focused on Earth as a force that is completely intertwined with our sustainability. The images of our reflections have been of danger and beauty, of new life and death. They very quickly have become mirrors for our joys and sorrows, our successes, our failures, and our transformations. The paradoxes found in our sensory environments allowed us to experience their many edges, challenging ourselves and one another to explore the deepest places of identity, self-definition, leadership, and spirituality. Talking openly about the paradoxes we faced and how we coped with them was, for us, a powerful experience; it was one of the keys to whether we—women who lead—merely survive or really thrive.

Ritual

The concept and process of ritual was another central component of our retreat circle and a tool that we used to focus ourselves personally as well as between and among each other as a group. A ritual is defined as "a rite, a ceremony, a series of symbolic acts focused toward fulfilling a particular intention . . . Rituals are an integral part of nature and our daily lives" (Beck & Metrick, 1990, p. 5). In essence, a ritual is something done formally in the physical realm—from a simple gesture of the hand to an elaborate ceremony—that relates to the higher worlds. The formality of rituals can vary dramatically. Rituals can be as elaborate as a black-tie awards dinner or as routine as working consciously in everyday life so that quite mundane tasks become infused with meaning. Although elements of ritual may be personal, this work is best done in communion with others. The ability to develop and share in rituals is important for personal growth as well as for cohesion and institutional memory of the group or organization. During our retreats, rituals were gentle and engaging—allowing each person to participate to the degree she felt able and safe. The sharing was intense, insightful, and very fruitful.

From our opening and closing ceremonies to our meals and to various daily exercises, we incorporated ritual throughout our time together, and we increasingly experienced its value. In one participant-facilitated celebration, we were in a beautiful grassy setting. We began by honoring Earth, Sky, and the Four Directions (East, South, North, and West) by facing each direction in turn, beginning with the East. We scooped up the energy of Earth with our hands, moving the energy through our bodies and then releasing that energy to the Sky. We did the exercise four times, as each of the Four Directions has its own metaphoric meaning and reality. (See Cross-Trainings, p. 15) By becoming aware of the energy of Earth and embodying it within ourselves, we were reminded that we are one with Earth and each other.

As in the retreats, the aspect of ritual has a place in our daily life, because it seeks to illuminate and connect the inner life with the outside world. Ritual is a way of being with self and others that allows for a perceptual shift in the understanding and meaning of connection; in fact, the presence of ritual celebration is a signpost of a healthy community that allows for "the coordination of human affairs with the great liturgy of the universe" (Berry, 1999, p. 17).

In our lives, the development of simple rituals, for example, a luncheon each month where people "catch up" with one another, can be both nonthreatening and inclusive. For us, the process of "checking in" at the beginning of all of our retreats provided the context for our participation. Moreover, sharing what was most important right then, what was uppermost in our minds and hearts—the joys and the sorrows—allowed others to more fully see and be with us, enabling each individual to be less distracted and more mindful during our precious time together.

Another ritual that we used to create our retreat community and bring all points of view into our meetings and gatherings was the Invitation Method (Law, 1993, p. 82). Using this approach, each member of the group invites another by name to share their ideas and opinions. It brings to consciousness the voices that are not usually heard. This is especially useful when there are people in a group who struggle to feel that their ideas are important. Having all our voices heard and acknowledged is a very important way to create that safe and supportive habitat for which we all long.

Seeds of Writing: Birthing of the Book

From the start, we learned incredible things during our time together. The power of our reflections and insights was so strong that we realized we could not contain our inquiry solely within ourselves. Our enthusiasm bubbled over, and we began to share our work with others. In so doing, we discovered more women leaders who expressed interest in the project, and our circle expanded. We began conducting interviews and hosting small group discussions with these friends and colleagues to explore issues that we had in common. As we carried these gifts back into our retreats, our feelings of affirmation and community grew exponentially. The names and roles of some of those women who joined us are listed at the end of this book as a way to publicly say thank you. Even with this, though, we really cannot thank them enough for their generosity of time, the careful articulation of their thoughts and feelings, and the courage to take this journey together.

At the conclusion of our fourth retreat, we found ourselves at an interesting and somewhat unexpected juncture. Through this work, we had gathered hundreds of pages of data, yet we realized that we were of many minds regarding our next steps. Many ideas for how to share the lessons from our experiences were generated during our time together. It also became clear that, although we had originally planned to co-create a book, the process of thematically analyzing and interpreting the vast amount of data that we had collected was a much more time-consuming and energy-intensive effort than we antic-ipated at the start, especially for nine women already working as hard as they could to balance their work, family, and other life commitments. In the end, four of us chose to move forward with the book project, the product of which is in your hands. The others elected to express the fruits of our retreat time spent together in different ways.

To further develop our story, those of us who chose to pursue the book continued to meet in retreats and conduct semistructured interviews and focus groups with other women to both more thoroughly explore our leadership roles and to address the issues of spirituality in depth. In the initial retreats, spirituality became more of an underlying current that flowed through our work rather than a concept, feeling, or practice that we investigated directly. Moving *Sustaining Our Spirits* to this next level of discovery was enlightening and also totally exciting as we once again continued to hear similar expe-riences and themes.

At this time, a fifth woman joined our circle as a research assistant and respondent to our conversations. Eventually, she has become a full participant with us, and what you read in these pages is as informed and shaped by her perspectives and experiences as by those of the many others who have shared their stories with us.

With the change in the composition of our retreat group came the change in dynam-ics as we moved into this new phase of exploration. Some of us who were more reticent in our first year of retreat began to become more active participants through verbal and written sharing, and some of us who had spoken quite a bit started to balance our ex-pression with more time for deep listening to others. What remained unchanged was our commitment to maintaining the inquisitive, introspective, creative, challenging, and mutually supportive atmosphere that had nurtured each of us so positively in our first four retreats. Our new sessions included deep reflection on those retreats as we sought to better understand and apply the lessons that they generated for us. We knew that the initial retreats had indeed been instrumental. They brought us together and focused our attention on the critical issues associated with women leaders' sustainabil-ity. We came to understand our initial retreat gatherings and the data generated not as the sole content for the book but rather as its context. The earlier retreats during which we explored the issues that women face as leaders were part of the ground upon which we built our relationships and our shared vision. They were the catalyst that allowed us to transform our ideas and experiences into something greater that we could share with others. In short, even as the nine original partners went in separate directions following the four retreats, we realized that the gift of these gatherings was a beginning, not an ending. They provided us with the balance and energy we needed to start uncovering and then disseminating the story of the leadership journey of women. We came to understand the initial retreats as manifestations of the connections and meanings that make up life itself, and, unexpectedly, they became both central to our discussion and the mechanism for our dialogue.

At the same time, these initial retreats were periods of such valuable personal growth that we had been unable to devote the time needed to processing the broader, commu-nal lessons. Now, we needed to create the space for both. Our subsequent retreats became safe places for gathering and releasing, for deepening and broadening, for pulling to-gether, breaking apart, and recombining anew our individual and group learnings for better understanding our own realities and those in the world beyond.

So once again, we met in retreats and further documented women's leadership stories. We continued to frame our work around the three research questions about threats and sustainability, and we continued to utilize a networking methodology to identify and interview additional women. Women we knew as leaders introduced us to women they knew and saw as leaders, who in turn led us to other women leaders, until we had been gifted by hours and hours of narratives and reflections from over 40 women in leadership roles. These women were chief executive officers, executive directors, and presidents, as well as chief academic officers, independent consultants, tribal chiefs, editors-in-chief, community elders, musicians, and visual artists. What we heard from these new colleagues resonated with our journeys; there was a kinship around the frustrations and the triumphs.

> *Leadership is a hard thing to talk about: you can't touch it; you know it when you see it; when you ask people to describe it or tell you about it, it's kind of hard to put into words, but you know it when you see it. Other things will happen when the leader figures out who they are and what makes them strong . . . and [are] not afraid to show their weaknesses and to tap into others.*
>
> **(Interviewee)**

We are excited about the prospect of continuing to hear and learn from women throughout the country. We felt it was imperative to translate what we had gleaned, and we did not want to take the next decade to share our thoughts and excitement with you. That being said, this work is so important to us and to the future of women that we hope this book will serve as a platform from which to broaden this inquiry even further—through you, your sisters, and your colleagues. The collective lessons revealed in this book were born from this rich history and share this ambitious goal.

When we began exploring the challenges, hopes, thrills, and realities of leadership through *Sustaining Our Spirits,* we focused our attention in three main areas. First, we wanted to understand some of the beliefs, practices, and resources that make us, as women, want to be leaders and keep us going every day in our leadership roles. Grounded in the power of this discovery, we sought to discern the elements in ourselves, our lives, our workplaces, and our world that are toxic to us, the characteristics and conditions that pose threats to our sustainability, the overt and underlying forces that put us in danger every day and over the long term. Finally, we began to consider the world as we hoped it would be for the women coming after us. We simultaneously looked inward and outward to discover what we needed more of in order for women like us to thrive as leaders—now and into the future.

One of our first challenges was to decide what and how to share this with you to most effectively bring you into our circle. After much thinking, discussion, and discernment, we made the decision to share our lessons as they clustered around overarching themes. To further validate each of our individual journeys, we wanted to tell at least part of the story in the words of women, like you, who are living this life every day. We have done this by augmenting the narrative with quotes from retreat participants and interviewees. As you have already seen, many of these quotes are offered as sidebars; some are included in the text. We decided early on that content would take precedence in selecting quotes. Each makes a statement on its own. Yet in most cases, although the words might differ, the thoughts and feelings they express are emblematic of the thoughts and feelings of many others. As such, although words from each speaker have been included, we elected not to identify them. We have, as mentioned earlier, listed their names in our acknowledgments at the end of the book. Rather than focus on who said what and when, we wanted to communicate the meaning behind the message. With these words, we hope to value the uniqueness of each individual leader while we also respect and pay homage to our shared story as women and as leaders who are finding ways to survive and thrive. Through our retreats, interviews, and analyses, we have enacted the position of "passionate participant" (Guba & Lincoln, 1994, p. 115), facilitating the "multi-voice" reconstructions (our own and the women who shared their stories) and even each of us as a "transformative intellectual" speaking as an advocate and activist toward expanding consciousness and transforming hegemony (Giroux, 1998, as cited in Guba & Lincoln, 1994, p. 115).

Please know that to be true to our experiences and the data gathered through our retreats and structured individual interviews and focus groups, this book's story about the dimensions of women leaders and the role of spirituality is not exhaustive. Despite the temptations to add material from new and relevant books and movies and to listen to all related tapes and songs, we have resisted. This may frustrate some of you, but we trust that most of you will applaud our efforts to be evidence-based.

To make the story of our journey even richer, we have included backstories throughout chapters 4 through 11, following our introduction. These sections add in-depth personal reflections and descriptions of our retreats and work as lived by us. The backstories offer a more comprehensive context to frame the narrative and, much like the sidebars, they provide a level of detail that we hope will make the themes come even more alive. Finally, we have included suggestions for deepening your experience of this book in "Cross-Trainings for the Soul." These sections offer additional readings, questions for reflection, and rituals that each of us can incorporate into our routines and into our leadership. Again, we could not list all the wonderful resources that are available to us, and we certainly do not presume that every resource listed will appeal to you equally. Nonetheless, we present a range of selections (with which at least one of us has had experience), and we hope that you will share with us and others the resources you have found helpful on your path as a leader.

We have grouped our chapters into two parts. Part 1 introduces the *Sustaining Our Spirits* initiative, our spiritual leadership paradigm, and the Earthview. Part 2 addresses the three questions that we asked: What sustains us as leaders? What threatens or challenges our sustainability? What wisdom do we want to pass on to the women coming after us? In it, we share our learnings, offer words of guidance for acting and aspiring women leaders, and seek to nourish the souls of all the women leaders who yearn for and are open to greater learning, growing, and more sustainable spirits. We then close the book with a short Epilogue—reminders from this time together, our shared experience, as we re-enter our places of work.

Each of us engages with the world in unique ways. Therefore, it is possible, indeed expected, that each woman, each leader, who reads this book will respond to it differently. Whatever feelings it evokes—validation, frustration, anger, hope,—our desire is that you can positively harness the power of these feelings and use them to shape your ongoing development. Only by acknowledging and building on our strengths as women and as leaders can we move forward to create a more generous and sustainable world.

As is evident by now, this book is our best interweaving of head, heart, and soul. We cover a lot of ground moving through past and current literature, from multiple perspectives to experience, lessons learned, wisdom, and the quiet voice within shared by women who lead in all sectors of our community—public, private, and nonprofit. We offer a new way of understanding leadership, by both showing the relationships that make up the whole and rearranging the known pieces to allow us to see them differently.

Yes, the *Sustaining Our Spirits* journey has been much longer and more complex than any of us initially imagined. But the process has become even more exciting and alive as the exploration of our individual leadership and spirituality has intensified through the ongoing conversation and as it continues to be reflected back to us through the prism of others. Our conversations together have revealed peculiarities as well as cultural and learned individualities; they have also demonstrated reassuring connections of shared vision, passion, frustrations, and delights among us as women. They have encouraged us and affirmed that this work is important. What do you dream for in this world? How do you want the planet to be for your grandchildren, their grandchildren, and all those women who come after us? Whatever your vision, it is imperative that we do all we can now to ensure a strong and nourishing habitat within ourselves, in our organizations, and in our communities.

We hope our book helps advance this vital work. As authors we share an enthusiastic commitment to the publication of this book, and we know we were blessed to find a publisher in NASW Press, the professional discipline of two of us. This Press (as is true for the national association) also believes in the importance of the process and the product of our journey. Within its own leadership, there happen to be strong and courageous women. Together, we are dedicated to disseminating the messages of this book and promoting ongoing dialogue and action around it. Now as we share our learnings with you, we also share our hope of honoring women leaders from the past, sustaining women leaders in the present, and inspiring women leaders for the future, for us all, our organizations, and, ultimately, for the world.

Cross-Trainings for the Soul

READINGS

- Angeles Arrien is a cultural anthropologist and cross-cultural teacher who has gleaned wisdom from many societies on how to meet and work with conflict, as well as the many ways to embrace conflict to make oneself a stronger, more effective leader. Her book, *The Four-fold Way: Walking the Paths of Warrior, Teacher, Healer and Visionary* (1993), is particularly powerful. Additionally, her Web site offers an overview of her work, along with a calendar of events: http://www.angelesarrien.com.

- Ted Andrews's (2006) *Animal Speak: The Spiritual and Magical Powers of Creatures Great and Small* also offers insights into the connection we, as humans, have with other beings on Earth.

- The Forum on Religion and Ecology, codirected by Mary Evelyn Tucker and John Grim, offers numerous resources on the connections between and among spirituality, religion, and Earth. Visit the Web site: http://www.religionandecology.org/About/founders.php.

REFLECTIONS

- What metaphor describes leadership for you? What lessons and actions are implied in that metaphor that can facilitate your development? Find a symbol that reminds you of that metaphor and revisit its richness and nuances every day to learn what it can teach you. An excellent article to help you think about leadership through metaphor is "Reimagining Our Academic Journeys Through Spiritual Metaphor" in the *Advancing Women in Leadership Journal* by Michelle Collay, Sandy Gehrig, Valerie Lesniak, and Carol Mayer (2002). In this article, four women in academia examine their separate and collective journeys through the use of the spiritually grounded metaphors of pilgrimage; labyrinth; gestation, birth, and rebirth; perpetual migration; and sisterhood.

- Consider our three research questions for yourself: What sustains you as a leader? What threatens you? What would you want to share with leaders to come? You may even want to share this conversation with a friend or convene a group of women you respect and facilitate a dialogue around these questions, much as we did. It can be a single session or you may elect to continue it, whichever feels most beneficial to you. Reflect on what you learn from this conversation and, as a result, what action, no matter how small, that you might take to nurture your spirit.

RHYTHMS & RITUALS

- Journaling is helpful to keep us reflecting on our daily experiences and making the connections that support our ongoing growth. Journaling provides us the feedback we might need to change course or keep the course in a leadership situation. It can take many forms. The key is to find the method that works for you. You might write an ongoing letter to yourself or to someone you love; you might write in a free-form style, essentially brainstorming whatever comes to mind; you might chronicle thoughts and feelings from your day. The approach does not matter as much as finding the way that best helps you document your history and reflect on your journey. It is also helpful to write down those thoughts that continue to run through your mind while you attempt to do other things! Books and tapes by the following authors offer resources for journaling: Clarissa Pinkola Estés, Marion Woodman, Linda Schiese Leonard, June Singer, and Sylvia Brinton Perera. All can be found at Amazon.com or online under the author's name. Audio recordings can be found at http://www.soundstrue.com.

- Expose yourself to new ideas regularly. Periodicals such as *Spirituality and Health, Real Simple, Science and Spirit, Explore: The Journal of Science and Health,* and *Magistra* contain many articles about the mind-body-spirit connection. They can be purchased at the newsstand and accessed online at http://www.SpiritualityHealth.com.

Spiritual Leadership for Our Organizations of the Future

'And what is as important as knowledge?' asked the mind.
'Caring and seeing with the heart,' answered the soul.

—Anonymous, as shared by Joyce McFarland

Leadership Skills

Attaining a position of leadership—the ability to use power for the good—is the ambition of many women. Leadership theory and practice have developed gradually over the past century. The ever-increasing number of women in organizational leadership roles further contributes to the evolution of the leadership landscape and its future. Yet for countless women who reach this pinnacle of success, traditional organizations built on Western cultural norms often feel artificial and even false. Despite the positive changes brought about over the years that have improved working conditions and increased productivity, the majority of these organizations can seem disjointed and fragmented. Often, the focus on efficiency and cost savings overwhelms people, making authentic relationships and the value that comes from them almost impossible to achieve. Streamlining, repositioning, rightsizing—these terms have frequently become euphemisms for doing more with less. Although some economic benefits may accrue through these changes in our organizations, as leaders we must question whether the financial gains warrant the concomitant losses in how we relate to and connect with each other, and, if so, what we are going to do about it.

> *Maybe I can say leadership is a process of learning about myself. I discover my own strengths and weaknesses by leading others. It's an educational path for me that surprises me. I find out more about myself through others.*
>
> **(Interviewee)**

Many organizations today seem to be a collection of people operating within their own domains, rather than a domain of people collectively operating. Leaders seem content to bring people together for periodic updates or in the face of specific problems without much attention to building unity or cohesion among them. People are continually cut off from each other in their places of work. Although not the sole sources of blame, the availability and accessibility of continual advancements in technology have greatly contributed to this social disconnect, emphasizing the solitary silos in which people can perform their jobs in virtual isolation, removed from the rest of the organization and with rarely an opportunity to connect or even interact with each other. The Internet—e-mails, blogs, podcasts, chat rooms, and other mass postings—has supplanted personal contact as the primary mode of communicating and transacting business. Telecommuting has revolutionized how we work. There are clearly advantages to the technology revolution, which has allowed our reach to extend across the globe in just seconds, but this form of contact may paradoxically also threaten the communal element of organizational life by serving to further separate us from each other. How many times have you experienced the breakdown in online communication that occurs without the intonations and nonverbal cues that accompany face-to-face conversations?

When everyone worked side by side, social events were a regular feature. Now this relational aspect of workplace culture has all but disappeared. Meetings have been replaced by online in-boxes full of daily and even hourly messages that require extensive engagement with the computer. Conversations around the watercooler have all but vanished in favor of instant messages that involve a new written language, an expedient and visual one, based almost entirely on abbreviations and symbols and universal "personal touches." All many of us need to do our jobs is a scope of work, a cell phone, and access to the World Wide Web. In fact, one "smart" phone would even allow you to download your job description! Yes, in spite of the benefits, these are some of the overt and underlying costs of just this single organizational advancement. As well described by Dilenschnieder (2007), to even survive in this world of technology, we must "accept, adapt, and accelerate—or atrophy" (p. 15) because "the new technologies are the door to the future" (p. 185).

Knowing what, when, and how to best use these technology innovations is only one component of effective leadership for the future. Discussed in much of the leadership literature, there are additional basic, yet critical, skills that leaders must possess and continually develop through knowledge and experience.

ANALYZING AND SYNTHESIZING

Throughout life, we are often encouraged to discern the discreet parts and differences between entities; we "analyze." Although this way of seeing has its own merit, in our "flat" (Friedman, 2005) and globalized world, we must also synthesize and look holistically to "connect the dots," to see the connections—as well as the differences—between and among us all so that we are better able to cross boundaries and reconceptualize relationships within the entire Earth community (Pink, 2005).

BENCHMARKING

Also known as *setting priorities*, benchmarking reflects the leader's values and directs behaviors by letting people know what is desired (Maciariello, 2006). Benchmarking establishes "controls" and must therefore focus on results, timeliness, and alignment with the goals, using qualitative and quantitative measures.

BUDGETING AND RESOURCE DEVELOPMENT

Together, budgeting and resource development provide primary tools for aligning plans and actions and also provide a framework for achieving accountability by evaluating existing products, processes, and programs for continuation and for forecasting results and future developments.

COLLABORATING

The most effective collaborating is truly co-laboring. It is the skill (and art and value) of working together. It requires that we continually communicate—to listen deeply and articulate clearly. It is a reciprocal process in which the roles of the initiator and receiver are traded back and forth.

CREATING

Creating actually involves a mindful understanding and appreciation of paradox. As Sorensen (2005) states, "One mark of a paradox is that different thinkers 'solve' it in incompatible ways. A strange mark of a paradox is that one and the same thinker 'solves' it in incompatible ways" (p. 299). Creating is seeing the "mind patterns" that have not been seen before (Eadie, 1998, p. 39). It is also about building—using the necessary time and resources to improve an organization and "[foster] an ethical culture" (Kolditz, 2007, p. 2). In particular, leaders of today's spiritual organizations must learn how to build and sustain interorganizational partnerships.

DECISION MAKING

Simply put, decision making is a skill and a practice that distinguishes leaders from all others in the organization. Peter Drucker (1966) has often reminded us that effective decisions are a hallmark of effective leaders. To enact this skill, it is important that we first define the issue and determine whether or not we really need to make a decision. Once we have clarified this, we must figure out whether we must deal with problems and/or dilemmas. Problems are either/or issues with right/wrong solutions. Dilemmas are a bit more complicated; they are composed of both/and issues that require the management of competing truths. Leadership for today and tomorrow has many more dilemmas to manage than problems to resolve.

After determining the type of issue, the leader's next step is to make the decision and convert the decision into action. Smart leaders then actively solicit feedback from their colleagues and, finally, evaluate both the decision and process. All in all, decision making is not a linear, neat process but is usually iterative and can be reiterative.

DEVELOPING AND EVALUATING SELF AND OTHERS

As Maciariello (2006) says, "One cannot develop oneself unless one is actively engaged in the development of others" (p. 20). As leaders, we need to continue to learn in order to improve ourselves, which will, in turn, enhance organizational growth.

MANAGING TIME

As leaders, we need to know how to balance competing demands, workload, and deadlines with energy. Managing time requires that we understand ourselves and our priorities, managing our own expectations, as well as the time demands placed on others.

RECOGNIZING AND REWARDING

The skills of recognizing and rewarding increase self-esteem and the motivation to perform effectively. They also offer new insights for the people performing the appraisal to better define jobs, clarify organizational goals, facilitate communication within the organization, and improve the operations of human resources.

STRATEGIC PLANNING

Strategic planning seeks to strike a balance between the organization's goals and resources and the external environment(s), and it aims to improve flexibility and adaptability in rapidly changing environments. It requires that we integrate new forms of technology as necessary, so that our organizations can remain nimble and develop along with a continually transforming world.

BEING TECHNOLOGY SAVVY

In today's globalized world in which technological developments occur at an almost inconceivably rapid pace, it is critical that leaders and their organizations stay abreast of the way that technology can enable them to operate and interact with others. To navigate through the volume of changing options, leaders must ensure that they do their research to elect the most appropriate technology for their organizations, customized with their personal touch (Dilenschneider, 2007).

> *Pulling women together to discuss spirituality, sustenance, and breath has been a dream from way back . . . pulling together women who are dealing with the same issues and who have developed strategies that are not written about in textbooks . . . I always talk about spirit when I discuss leadership. People are starting to get it. Exploring this connection allows us to delve more deeply into something that helps us be who we are.*
>
> **(Retreat participant)**

VISIONING

Visioning articulates an aspiration, an open invitation; it goes beyond what is missing and speaks to what can be. From the vision, all else follows—the organization's mission (or reason for being) and then the strategic priorities and actions to be taken.

As leaders, we can likely identify other skills that we need in our roles. In general, however, developing and utilizing these skills create organizations with what is known for being referred to as a "high spirit of performance" led by those who have a deep and sustained commitment to doing what is right to get done what is right. As Drucker reminds us, organizations become great when their leadership is great—when their leaders embody this spirit of performance.

Spirituality

Although it is very important, developing skills in these areas does not complete our task to most effectively move forward; we must lead holistically, publicly embracing and enacting both traditional skills and what is most recently referred to as "spiritual leadership" skills (Bailey, 1997, 2006; Bailey & Uhly, 2008; Bolman & Deal, 1995). Only as we move through the continuous process of integrating head and heart are we able to fulfill our personal and organizational needs.

Out of the thousands published, with few exceptions, the vast majority of academic textbooks and popular literature in the twentieth century have not considered spirituality as a central component of leadership. It was not until the 1990s that an increasing focus on interconnection and some of the inherent elements of spirituality made their way into publications on leadership. Titles like *The Fifth Discipline: The Art and Practice of the Learning Organization* (Senge, 1990); *The Active Life: A Spirituality of Work, Creativity, and Caring* (Parker, 1990); *Leading with Soul: An Uncommon Journey of Spirit* (Bolman & Deal, 1995); and *Leadership in a Challenging World: A Sacred Journey* (Shipka, 1997), began appearing on bookstore shelves. Now we find more, including "Successful Women Leaders: Achieving Resiliency Through Rituals and Resources" (Detrude & Stanfield, 2000), *A Dream and a Plan: A Woman's Path to Leadership in Human Services* (Gardella & Haynes, 2004); *Resonant Leadership: Renewing Yourself and Connecting with Others Through Mindfulness, Hope, and Compassion* (Boyatzis & McKee, 2005); and *Theory U: Leading from the Future as it Emerges* (Scharmer, 2007). Even though each of these authors approaches spirituality a bit differently, they and we concur that spirituality is the force that breathes life into every being on Earth.

Beyond any formal definition, spirit is almost universally recognized by women leaders as our connection to the greater world. It is the energy that weaves throughout our relationships. Despite growing attention to the subject of spirit, the discussion of leadership in the context of spirituality is still not the norm. Not many conversations on this topic can be overheard in boardrooms or even lunchrooms. However, in the safe, nurturing presence of people in whom we trust, women reveal much about the vital role that spirituality plays in their lives and their work, whether or not they use the specific term.

Throughout *Sustaining Our Spirits,* the concept of spiritual leadership resonated with us, and we affirmed that spirituality is what weaves together the elements of our lives to help support and sustain us, personally and professionally, as authentic leaders in our organizations.

The concept of spirituality has undeniably been central to our discussions as we focused on our sustainability—how we live, grow, and thrive. Across all sectors, the women leaders that we interviewed consistently referenced the concept of spirituality as a sustaining force in their lives and in their successes. Indeed, studies have shown that people who claim to have a high degree of spirituality are healthier than those that do not (Nagel, 2007). Nevertheless, it took us considerable time and reflection to fully elucidate the meaning of spirituality and derive a definition that resonated for us.

> *There is an energy that we tap into . . . It's an energy that keeps the universe going. And to keep it going, we have to tap into it. Through our leadership, we're sustaining that energy and giving it back.*
>
> **(Interviewee)**

The ancient meaning of the term spirituality is something that transcends the material world: it is something that we can experience, but cannot see; spirituality is something that people can experience but not literally see or hold (Kurtz & Ketcham,

2002). For us and for the women we interviewed, spirituality transcends religion and goes beyond religious affiliation. For many, their religious selves and their relationships with God or a supreme power are part of their spirituality, but there is more: it has as much to do with relationships, particularly their roles in promoting and supporting the best in them.

Exploring definitions of spirituality was just the first step for us; agreeing on a definition of spirituality to offer in this book was the next step and a bit more challenging. We did it by going back to what we have relied on throughout the entire *Sustaining Our Spirits* process. We looked for references, we reflected, we shared stories, and we kept listening to the voices of the women who entered our circle. Eventually our definition surfaced. We knew it when we felt confident that it encompassed the richness of all we had read and heard.

For us, spirituality is the connective tissue that joins our thoughts, our actions, and our purpose. In fact, its Latin root, *spiritus*, literally means "breath" or "breath of life." As a unique individual, each person is a "creature who acts, thinks, and feels. Spirituality fuses these three into a single reality" (Chopra, 2004, p. 3), therefore providing the impetus to lead, create, and be ourselves holistically. Spirituality is intimately related to the destiny of all, representing "a personal and communal quest for a sense of wholeness and/or connection to the divine" (Cady, 2006, p. 22). And while it is easy to consider spirit separate from work, this intimate relationship means spirit connects us to everyone in our organizations and reminds us that all of our actions, however seemingly big or small, impact all of us. Its manifestations for our souls and our organizations lie at the core of our path toward shared discovery and success, connecting the past to the future. Often, we do not recognize it is there until we are reminded.

> I experience spirituality when feeling connection and discovery of communities that I don't see every day. . . . At the College, I met an alum who is 93 years old; she tells me that [the College] was the only one to let black folks in to be teachers when she was young and it spawned generations of people who value education in her family . . . It's these moments that remind me of how interrelated our lives really are.
>
> **(Retreat participant)**

By fortifying our internal, our personal, resources and cultivating our inner core where all of our strengths and capacities are integrated, we enhance our ability to more meaningfully and deeply connect with others. We are better able to recognize that we have a responsibility to respond to others and to use our gifts in the greater context of our interconnected life, rather than simply for our own pleasure or advancement.

From this perspective, we begin to see that our leadership is best understood as emanating from a center of our organizations and rippling throughout them. It is not driven from the top, as Western organizations typically depict it or even, as characteristic of Greenleaf's (1977) servant leadership, rising up from the bottom. Because of our inherent interconnectedness, the center is more a conceptual starting point than a physical location. Leadership guided by the spirit taps into the invisible web that runs through and connects everyone. When leaders acknowledge an organization's

> *I think that spirituality comes from within. It has to do with your sense of connection with the wider world around you and the world that we can't put our finger on. It has to do with your inner core and who you are deep inside. It does connect to a greater life, power, something . . . Hopefully, it shows up in the way we make decisions, the things that we become involved in, our relationships, and it centers us in terms of giving us perspectives of who we are in the world around us. We don't do things in a vacuum. The spiritual part comes out in our involvement with the world . . . To me, that means that we have to be in touch with the fact that who we are touches everything around us. Who we are is involved with everything out there, and we don't exactly know what that all is . . . We are all connected in some way. Our spirituality allows us to connect and to feel that. That's how I see myself. I don't see myself as someone out there by myself doing my thing because of my sense of being a part of a greater context and my spirituality.*
>
> (Interviewee)

humanity, they can invite the whole to engage in the co-construction of new possibilities, fostering alignment with the spiritual energy, or connectedness. Accordingly, the process of sustaining our spirits as leaders and as women within our organizations and communities requires us to be and to act in ways that foster relationship, reflection, maintenance, adaptation, and innovation.

The concepts of spirituality and soul that we posit here, again, clearly extend beyond traditional religious practice. Whereas religion originates in external institutions and practices, which can sometimes separate and divide, spirituality is a centering force that comes from within, which can unify. Consistent with Rolheiser's (1999) broader descriptions,

> Spirituality is more about whether or not we can sleep at night than about whether or not we go to church. It is about being integrated or falling apart, about being within the community or being lonely, about being in harmony with Mother Earth or being alienated from her . . . What shapes our actions is our spirituality. (p. 7)

Likewise, the soul is a complex and vital energy that shapes and both sets us apart and connects us with each other. "Our soul is not something we have; it is more something we are. It is the very life-pulse within us. The soul not only makes us alive . . . it also makes us one" (Rolheiser, 1999, pp. 12–13).

In truth, these eloquent definitions have provided a foundation to begin our journey to understand spirituality and leadership, but they are still not complete in and of themselves. Spirituality is not just about being integrated at the risk of being separated; sometimes, it involves falling apart as preparation for real integration. Isolation or time

On the personal side, I must be grounded in my spirituality and health so that psychologically I'm rested, so that spiritually I'm grounded. There is a regular kind of meditation or reflection that keeps me grounded. The other part of that is that the spiritual practice also involves other people—community. There's a spiritual practice that I do that involves a small community and we do this practice together, and I am always experiencing something beautiful out of that. I have to make sure that it happens and that I place myself in that community to think together and support each other and meditate, and that's one thing.

(Interviewee)

alone can be necessary for us to bring our authentic selves to community. And sometimes, true alienation establishes the longing for harmony with nature and Earth that leads us to live truly connected lives that establish harmony with our world. We must attend to our inner lives at the same time that we interact with others; spirituality is both an inner journey as well as an engagement with community.

To be effective leaders, therefore, we must fulfill our spiritual needs, realizing that we can achieve spiritual nourishment through our connections with others as well as our attention to personal reflection and rejuvenation. Our spirituality makes up the well of reserves from which we draw during times of tension, allowing us to lead purposefully with energy and enthusiasm and preventing burnout. Spirit allows us to be "inspiring" leaders—literally "filling with spirit" those with whom we come in contact (Owen, 1999, p. 52). It is important as leaders that we ensure that our spiritual well is full by embracing the values and learning the additional competencies that allow us to focus and renew.

Undergirding the aforementioned characteristics and skills to ensure a more balanced, holistic enactment of leadership are actually seven leadership attributes that, when acknowledged, cultivated, and deployed, enable us all to challenge and push against the inequalities in our world to create organizations with a high spirit of performance; they strengthen our ability to lead from spirit (Bailey, 2006). In fact, recent studies have shown that organizations that seek to recognize the spirit and even attempt to align their goals with the spirit outperform those that do not (e.g., Mitroff & Denton's study as cited in Pink, 2005).

This set of core competencies—authenticity, humility, empathy, courage and compassion, faith, patience, and love—composes the "spirit" or the essence of life (Bailey, 2006). Although rarely discussed in the literature, these elements are critical for us to achieve integration and balance as leaders, and they offer a framework within which to support the twelve leadership skills that we discussed earlier.

AUTHENTICITY

Authenticity begins with self-discovery. As leaders, we must invest our time into finding out and genuinely knowing who we really are—understanding our gifts as well as those things that challenge us. This may require that we take the time to learn more about ourselves through self-discovery. We can truly understand our spirituality if we know who we really are, including our strengths and the areas that challenge us, and then purposefully, unabashedly express who we really are (Bailey, 2006). Each of us gifts the world with our presence, and it is our responsibility to be all we really are. Our individual actions compose the course of life on Earth, and our impact—although sometimes seemingly minimal—actually radiates from where we are in often unknown ways. It is therefore critical for us to act with integrity according to our being. Naturally, as we learn and grow through life, our beliefs

> *How do I deal with being authentic? It's not 'a dealing with' for me. It's the only way I know how to be.*
> **(Interviewee)**

may shift and evolve, yet authentic self-knowledge facilitates our ability to render authentic trust among the people with whom we interact, which further strengthens our connections with them and our organizations.

Once we have established this self-knowledge, we can most fully live into it, feeling grounded and acting with integrity. Indeed, research by Kusy and Essex (2007) suggests that leaders who are authentic are seen by others as most successful. This is most evident when leaders have made mistakes.

HUMILITY

Humility finds its root in the word *humus,* or earth. As mentioned earlier, it is a centeredness or grounding that one has in the world, which recognizes the transience of positional power and acknowledges that individual worth is more than a title or involvement with a particular project or organization. Genuine humility encourages leaders to build character by seeking beyond themselves and the need for approval from others at any cost. Humility contains its own paradox; to quote a Sufi saying, "A saint is a saint unless he knows that he is one" (Kurtz & Ketcham, 2002, p. 186).

EMPATHY

Empathy blossoms out of authenticity and humility as the space "to be able to 'hold' the perceptions and the emotions of another" (Bailey, 2006, p. 300), opening one's mind and heart to others while still being true to oneself. As leaders, we must be conscious of our ability to open up to others and be willing to do so.

COURAGE AND COMPASSION

As we have noted, leadership is challenging and is sometimes downright scary! In fact, the word *leadership* comes from the Indo-European root, *leith,* which means "to go forth," "to cross the threshold," or "to die" (Scharmer, 2007)—definitely not for the faint of heart! Certainly, then, courage and compassion are two critical components of leadership. We have combined these elements because they work best together and provide balance. With courage and compassion, leaders can make purposeful, definite, and strategic decisions while at the same time respecting the joys and struggles of others and appreciating the "big picture." They fortify leaders to embrace paradox, moderating the effects of stressors that might emerge as harmful to health (Sapolsky, 2004).

FAITH

As described by Bailey (2006), "The faith of leadership is about living with uncertainty and trusting that all that happens serves a higher good; that there is a lesson to be learned in every pleasure and every pain" (p. 300). Contrary to popular misconception, faith is not synonymous with religion. It does not abandon reason; it does not ignore people and situations that are dishonest or dangerous; it does not inhibit us from seeking and creating new knowledge. Faith can be the origin of inspiration, as well as the energy for hope during the daily grind. Often, faith serves as the foundation for organizations' most effective "vision" statements, as visions extend beyond the present into future possibilities.

Although most organizations develop and reference vision statements rather easily, faith is often difficult to sustain because fear often replaces it, especially with the constant changes and ambiguity in the world. Elements of fear will always be present throughout life, yet leaders must embrace faith and extend it to the others in their organizations as they move forward in the complexities of life (Morris, 2007).

PATIENCE

Patience is an active appreciation for the wisdom and processes of the Earth. It is the willingness to attend to ourselves and other people and situations, realizing that we must remain aware of the flow of life to take advantage of timing. Patience allows us to know and trust that, as Eccles. 3:1-8 reminds us, there is a season for everything.

LOVE

The love of a leader extends broader and wider than the love one holds for family and friends. This is the same love that is essential to the power of dialogue. This type of love, which leaders must help grow throughout their organizations is *agape.* Agape is a transcendent love for all beings, simply because they exist. It is the blending of authenticity, empathy, humility, courage and compassion, patience, and faith into a desire for active involvement to create a better future in a complex and multilayered way (Scharmer, 2007).

I think as individuals, we all have a responsibility to the world to use the gifts that we've been given to make it work and be a better place. That's part of my spirituality. I think that it's part of being alive. We are given gifts, and we have the responsibility to use them well.

(Interviewee)

In sum, these are seven of the critical competencies that collectively form a solid foundation for true and effective leadership in the interconnected world that we share. When we integrate them fully into our ways of relating as leaders in all aspects of our lives, we find we have the requisite skills and attitudes to manage the paradoxes we face daily as leaders and we have the capacity to create, thriving for ourselves and our organizations.

Cross-Trainings for the Soul

READINGS

- Diarmud O'Murchu's (2007) *Transformation of Desire: How Desire Became Corrupted and How We Can Reclaim It* is a wonderful resource on spirituality and its roots. The following offer perspectives on spirituality from a variety of faiths: *The Holy Longing* by Ronald Rolheiser (1999), *With Roots in Heaven: One Woman's Passionate Journey into the Heart of Her Faith* by Tirzah Firestone (1999), *A Prayer for Spiritual Elevation and Protection* by Muhyiddin Ibn 'Arabi (2006), *Be Here Now* by Ram Dass (1971), and *Teachings of Don Juan: A Yaqui Way of Knowledge* by Carlos Casteneda (1968).

- Consult any of the works of Jean Houston. See http://www.jeanhouston.org for information about her current works and programs, especially her efforts in meeting the challenges of globalization and culture through social artistry. Her published material includes guided meditation, enactment of great myths and stories, and practices to integrate the many aspects of our "polyphrenic" nature, including, for example, Houston's (1982) *The Possible Human: A Course in Enhancing Your Physical, Mental, and Creative Abilities.*

- Lest anyone think we are not recovering "technophobes," we also recommend the monthly magazine *Fast Company,* published by Manuscript Ventures, LLC. Geared for our corporate colleagues but with just enough well-written, highly creative articles and advertisements, it can stretch, delight, and excite us all! Learn more at http://www.fastcompany.com.

REFLECTIONS

- Reflect on your own leadership. What have been some of your highpoints? Recall one or two experiences that make you especially proud. What made them so special? How did they make you feel?

- What opportunities do you have to grow and develop as a leader? What skills might present new possibilities for you? What core competencies can you enhance? What can you do today?

- Think about the spiritual elements of leadership of authenticity, humility, empathy, courage and compassion, patience, faith, and love. Which attributes are at the "heart" of your leadership strengths? Which attributes would serve to strengthen your leadership skills needing attention?

RHYTHMS & RITUALS

- Listen to a variety of music; choose music that connects to your heart, head, and gut. Know what music energizes, relaxes, and creates a safe space around you. We have included the lyrics for two songs in the Appendix. "Come to Me in Prayer" was written by one of the women we interviewed, and "If I Were Brave" was cited by one of our interviewees as an incredibly powerful song that offers courage when she becomes frustrated or anxious. We hope that they will be of inspiration to you in this work.

- Explore ritual in Caroline Myss's (1996) *Anatomy of the Spirit: The Seven Stages of Power and Healing.* Myss has a number of books, tapes, and videos that help people to understand their way of working in the world. Her insight about people gives us information as to how to keep sustaining our spirit.

Leading Through the Earthview

Our personal attempts to live humanely in this world are never wasted.
Choosing to cultivate love rather than anger just might be what it takes
to save this planet from extinction.

—Pema Chödrön, *The Places That Scare You*

Our exploration into leadership skills and spirituality brought us to uncover another primary principle that further complemented and interwove throughout our thoughts, reflections, and understanding of our work. We call this the Earthview, a term that has been used by scientists, including NASA, when describing a holistic view of Earth. Although the foundation ideas of the Earthview have existed for much of the last half-century, only recently have they begun to be incorporated more prominently into thought and discussion of leadership and organizations.

Despite the reality of spirit, quite frequently our world has been dichotomized as eastern and western, north and south, indigenous and developing. In many cases, these distinctions serve little purpose beyond fueling a growing polarity between groups and cultures. At the same time, when viewed with an intention of understanding, they can be instructive descriptors that illustrate similarities and differences in styles that help us appreciate both. It is with this awareness that we broach just such an examination of organizational culture and leadership.

If we quickly peruse the management literature, we can see that a Western worldview dominates much of our organizational thinking, especially in the United States. Although new interpretations continue to shape how our organizations operate, a capitalist, free market philosophy grounds our leadership ethos.

> *As an artist and a leader, there is an awareness that I'm observing a truth that others might not see. As a creator, I can excavate a truth—as simple as it may be—one that I see that others may not see as clearly . . . It's healing.*
>
> **(Interviewee)**

Among its strengths, the Western approach promotes innovation and entrepreneurship and supports risk taking with the prospect of commensurate rewards. On the other hand, a fundamental assumption resides at the core of the Western worldview: Everything is separate. This assumption runs counter, or at least parallel, to our understanding of spirituality and does not allow much room for its expression. In the Western worldview, that is, in most of our Western organizations, individualism is highly prized. People who lead are singled out and given a high degree of freedom and authority to direct the actions of many. Correspondingly, the group's outcomes quite often are attributed directly to the leader without much consideration for others' roles. This may strike many as the way it should be, particularly when things do not turn out as envisioned. However, it becomes a concern for those same people when they are not appropriately recognized for their accomplishments. From a more universal perspective, actions like this threaten the integrity and sustainability of an organization or team. We do not have to look much beyond the growing disparity in compensation between the top executives of a business and its line staff to see additional evidence of some of the more disquieting impacts of the Western worldview on organizational life (see Table 1).

The Western view is further characterized by clearly delineated problems with right or wrong, simple answers to questions. In this world, things are either complementary to one another or oppositional. In these organizations, we spend more time identifying and fixing problems so we can control outcomes than we do cultivating our capacity for growth and possibility with the goal of greater efficiency for optimal effectiveness. The evolution of quality control practices, like Six Sigma, Lean Flow, and others, has created environments in which eliminating errors is the most important objective. In this environment, fear of failure tends to negate the opportunity to learn and grow. Rigid, narrow definitions reign, and everything can be ordered by its understood value. The higher something is hierarchically, the more importance it is given. Boundaries and roles are established to maintain separation and order. Relationships between the "higher" and "lower" rankings develop under a pretense of expert authority, although they often manifest as oppression or an exercise in control. Certainly visible in many of our Western organizations, this ordering for the purpose of domination extends beyond those with whom we work. It can also be seen clearly in our fervent attempts to control animals, plants, and even the natural forces alive in our world. Look how much time we spend trying to keep the weeds out of our yard or trying to "predict" the weather. By exerting authority, leaders attempt to create stability and avoid disorder in their organizations, yet many experience it as a force driving fragmentation and disintegration.

Table 1: Western Worldview

1. Everything is separate.
2. Order is hierarchical and ladderlike. Things valued as more important are ranked higher than those valued as less important.
3. Relationships are based on order and the illusion of control of higher orders over lower orders.

Note. Based on the work of Swimme, B., & Berry, T. (1992). *The universe story: From the primordial flaring forth to the ecozoic era—a celebration of the unfolding of the cosmos.* New York: Harper Collins.

Many Eastern and indigenous cultures espouse a more expansive worldview in which the ideas of interconnectedness and community are central and commonplace. This worldview is more consistent with a spirit-based approach to leadership. The Dalai Lama, for example, conceptualizes the interconnectivity of life in the universe as described in the ancient myth of Indra's net (Chan & His Holiness the Dalai Lama, 2004).

According to the story, the universe consists of a huge web of countless, interwoven strands of thread, and at each juncture is fastened a diamond (see Figure 1). Through its innumerable facets, each single diamond reflects light from all of the other diamonds in the net. Furthermore, vibrations in one part of the net initiate a ripple effect across the entire net, even ever so slightly. Universal connectivity is also a central tenet of Taoism, in which the Tao is a deep source of energy that flows through all beings. Even within the traditional Western theological context, the divine purpose of creation is to glorify the whole, rather than any single piece of the sum total (Berry, 1999).

Although definite differences exist between various tribal perspectives, many Native American cultures believe that human beings have a reciprocal relationship with the natural world, and many of their rituals involve interaction with Earth. Their conception of leadership is one of connection. In fact, the word *leadership* is not found in many of their languages (Simms, 2000). Rather, these native cultures espouse a belief in the simultaneity of leadership and followership wherein individuals lead when they are called to do so, with the real power drawn not from an individual person but rather from the community (McCleod, 2002; Simms, 2000).

In our very practical and visual world, it is a challenge to fathom the vastness of our interconnectivity. One way is to consider how Zen Buddhist monk Thich Nhat Hanh (1992) illustrates our inter-being: "If you are a poet, you will see that there is a cloud floating in this sheet of paper. Without the cloud, there will be no rain; without rain, the trees cannot grow; and without trees, we cannot make paper" (p. 95).

Another way is to really look at Earth. The first time we were able to do this was in 1969 when the National Aeronautics and Safety Administration (NASA) released its

I also have this sense that people, in general, seem to be hungry for connecting and moving out of this mechanistic linear world that we've been in since we left the agrarian economy and moved into the Industrial Age. We've been so linear, and there are so many changes on so many fronts now— quantum physics, metaphysics, integrated medicine—all kinds of things that people intuitively held to be true prior to modernization; now we're finding actual proof of them. I think people are hungry to get out of the mode and to get into a high level of connectivity.

(Interviewee)

Figure 1 Indra's Net

photographs of Earth taken from space (see Figure 2).

FIGURE 2   NASA Earthview (NASA)

This quintessential photo is relatively commonplace now. However, more recent satellite images of our remarkable planet continue to reinforce the realization made in 1969: Our place as human beings on this planet is intricately connected to every other place and every other being.

Furthermore, each member of Earth's community holds an integral role, contributing to the story of our planet—the cosmogenesis (Swimme & Berry, 1992). Now just imagine the ramifications of this for our organizations and our leadership!

Earth presents us with a different way of framing how leadership and organizations might function. Reflecting on our global interconnectedness, the Earthview enables us to draw on the primary principles from lessons grounded in the recognition of our life and experiences as part of a wholly collective ecosystem; views that are consistent with Eastern and indigenous philosophies and the way women tend to perceive the world. According to the Earthview, everything is connected. Rather than linear and hierarchical, order is circular and interdependent; everyone and everything contributes to the whole and shares an equality of value and belonging. Within the whole, individual perceptions are acknowledged and appreciated for the diversity that they contribute, yet are understood in relation to others. As such, everything can be both complementary and oppositional.

> *Figure out what your values are, and then do what you need to do to keep those intact . . . and to share those with others.*
>
> **(Interviewee)**

It might seem that such a focus on relationships and connectivity is largely subjective, but scientific findings are continuing to support this conception of the nature of life and actions. This broad sense of interdependency has been noted at a much more intimate scale in the field of quantum physics. The work of the German mathematician Amalie Emmy Noether (Noether's theorem) significantly contributed to the development of quantum physics, but it was Niels Bohr, the Danish physicist, who recognized the quality and complementarity in atomic structures and is credited for formulating its first quantum model. Since then, physicists have described even subatomic relations in terms consistent with those of the Earthview, asserting that what may seem to be opposite and contradictory is actually part of a deeper unity. Moreover, they have proved the reality of a cosmic "stickiness" through which objects that interact at one point remain in connection forever, yielding true quantum interconnectedness (Bell's theorem). This perspective views all space as relational and all interaction as influential. The connection on the quantum level reflects the interdependency throughout the universe (see Table 2).

The convergence of Western and Eastern philosophies is also being demonstrated in other scientific disciplines. Over the last 10 years, research in the fields of psychology

**Table 2: Cosmological Principles of the Earthview:
A Reflection-to-Praxis Process**

1. Everything is connected.

2. Order/hierarchy is circular. Everything is interdependent and interrelated as a valuable contribution to the whole. Human beings have a special role of choice and responsibility.

3. Rather than in a static existence, the universe continually unfolds and emerges in time and space. All creatures are part of this process. Once an event takes place, it is irreversible.

4. Participation in life is not a choice.

5. Life reacts to directives.

6. Human beings create their own interpretations of reality.

7. A living system becomes healthier by connecting it more to itself.

Note. Adapted from Swimme, B., & Berry, T. (1992). *The universe story: From the primordial flaring forth to the ecozoic era—a celebration of the unfolding of the cosmos.* New York: Harper Collins. (See also Senge, 1990; Wheatley, 1999.)

and neuroscience has been revealing much about the mind–body–spirit connection. We can now see the effects of positive and negative emotions on brain scans, and the healing benefits of compassion, mindfulness, and other practices more traditionally associated with Eastern thought have been documented. In all of this work, spirit is central regardless of whether or not it is defined that way. Dr. George Vaillant, a research psychiatrist and director of Harvard's seventy-year-long human lifetimes study, has done considerable research integrating studies of human and animal behavior. He states that "mammalian evolution has hard-wired the brain for spiritual experience . . . the most dramatic spiritual experience is joy. Developmentally, the child's smile, the kitten's purr, and the puppy's wagging tail emerge at the same time. These social responses are elicited by, and in turn elicit, positive emotion," whereas "negative emotions help us to survive individually; positive emotions help the community to survive. Joy, unlike happiness, is not all about *me*—joy is connection" (Lambert, 2007, p. 8). It follows then that joy is also at the heart of our leadership inquiry.

Similar messages of Eastern and Western "cross-fertilization" and the importance of cultivating positive mind states are described in Daniel Goleman's (2003) in-depth recounting of a seminal dialogue among Buddhist scholars, including the Dalai Lama, and Western psychologists, scientists, and philosophers that took place in March 2000. The purpose was to explore and consider ways to deal with our destructive emotions. Although many questions arose, the inquiry confirmed the importance of delving deeper into the understanding of the mind and its potential to help us live fuller, healthier, and more peaceful lives. As this work continues, we will open up new avenues for appreciating and enriching our selves and the communities we help to lead and to which we belong.

In truth, life is filled with relationships, and it is impossible to escape interaction. As Wheatley (2006) has written, "We are constantly creating the world—evoking it, not discovering it—as [we] participate in all its main interactions. This is a world of process, not a world of things" (p. 68). We have no choice but to participate in a world of such interconnectivity.

> *We have to be in touch with the fact that who we are touches everything around us. Who we are is involved with everything out there, and we don't exactly know what that all is. It comes down to things like being careful what you wish for, being thankful and satisfied for your life. . . . We are all connected in some way.*
>
> (Interviewee)

> *I think a leader is someone who earns and maintains the respect of a particular constituency—small, large, local, national, familial—from actions more than words, although words are also important . . . I think people who are looked upon as leaders are people in whom others have confidence and can get a particular job performed. A person who steps up to challenges, and takes responsibility for things, particularly when things go wrong and that person is the head or the 'go-to,' front-line person, who does not shirk that responsibility, that ownership of projects. So, a leader is the one who has to be willing to accept the bad things.*
>
> (Interviewee)

Within our web of connections, each living being is situated at a particular position within the web of life—at a juncture in Indra's net; although we each may reflect all of life, each of our perspectives is slightly different. Yearning to understand ourselves and our surroundings, we piece together events and contexts in ways that make sense to us and allow us to continue to interact with life's participants from our individual contexts. Through our interconnected engagement with others and our environment, whether fully intentional or not, we release energy and ideas that form the basis for our perceptions of the world and, in turn, shape the world itself. In doing so, we all creatively contribute to the diversity of ideas that exist with exciting and new potential implications for impacting our world.

Creation is an integral part of life's processes. Everywhere, potential exists for creative development, resulting in more and complex organisms. Through each passing moment, life continues to emerge, unfold, and transform in irreversible ways. Indeed, everything is affected by each action and inaction; because of the interdependency among beings, even if one undoes a specific action, it is impossible to undo or even calculate the ramifications of the original event. The concept of control does not fit within the Earthview, in part because life is far too complex and overwhelming to actually control; a change in one area has a myriad of ramifications throughout the system, no matter the scale. Just consider the well-known analogy of the butterfly effect: Every choice and action begets infinite consequences that have influence—great and small, good and bad, far and wide. The flap of a butterfly's wing in Texas can cause a tsunami in Japan, for instance. The impact of anything one does reaches far beyond the imagination.

Despite all of what we know to the contrary, because much of our daily life is built upon the assumptions of the Western worldview, most of us working in today's organizations interact with each other and the world in ways at least subtly governed by the dominating principles of separation and control. The entrenchment of bureaucracy and the prevalence of hierarchical organizational charts clearly give testament to the predominance of this paradigm. Typically, people and resources are conceived as discreet variables that can be added or subtracted to achieve distinct and calculated results, and this addition and subtraction model further reinforces separation and impersonal interaction with life. From the Western worldview mind-set, the Earthview concepts may seem a little bit unsettling, frustrating, or even frightening at first. Leaders are traditionally taught to plan and to control in order to achieve security (their own and that of others). Relinquishing the concept of control contradicts our attempts to protect ourselves and our organizations from uncertain outcomes.

> *The notion of creation is another belief of mine that has to do with leadership. I truly believe that every human heart that beats is a creative human being. It makes us human.*
>
> **(Interviewee)**

Nevertheless, striving to control outcomes builds false expectations and actually sets leaders and our organizations up for failure. Changing lenses to the Earthview perspective infuses the concept of connection into our understanding of leadership and organizational behavior. We must trust in the more organic and ever-evolving processes of life, allowing ourselves to be more adaptable and at peace with change. Through its connections and interactions, life on Earth—including organizations—is self-organizing. Although initially paradoxical, healthy organizations are mature systems that survive and even achieve a flowing stability by consistently fostering renewal and evolution and by supporting the effects of change throughout the system (Wheatley, 2006). Integration and full appreciation of each person and resource in the system encourage a holistic understanding of the organization and its management. These acts also engender feelings of belonging among individuals by stimulating engagement (Fris & Lazaridou, 2006). They are integral for strengthening our organizational systems and our own leadership.

Three of our four initial *Sustaining Our Spirits* retreats were held on a farm in the southeast United States. The fourth was held near the ocean. The retreat locations were intentionally selected. The settings brought us close to the natural cadences of Earth; we shared this space with animals, insects, flowers, plants, water, trees, and other people. We experienced the pull of the tides and the lunar cycle. We became aware of the need to make connections with Earth and her rhythms, the mysterious principles that govern all life on this planet. It was through our reflection on Earth that we began to link her fragile sustainability and the many toxins to which she has been subjected with our roles as women leaders.

Consider garbage, for example. It is not at the forefront of your mind when you are surrounded by pristine natural beauty and unconsciously drink water from a well or a stream, expecting it will be pure. Many of us do not give much thought to the one battery that we throw away because it is only one or the disposal of plastic containers from our microwaveable lunches, which at least offer us some semblance of a healthy meal during our hectic days. Yet as these products break down in our landfills, which contain many other similar items, they release toxins that leach into the soil and have the potential to contaminate our water, our food, and our bodies.

The same principle applies to us as leaders. Seemingly small actions can be harmful, and disharmonies and negative emotions can accumulate until our bodies and our organizations start to break down. Just as we need to take steps to maintain a healthy water supply, we also need to actively promote healthy leadership for healthy organizations.

When we fully comprehend that all is one, we are automatically connected to everyone and everything. In our *Sustaining Our Spirits* retreats, we became aware that this proposition was the necessary backdrop for our work. Many of us were feeling confined as leaders trying to operate within and often at odds with our Western-style organizations. We had a choice to view our leadership differently, and by making this choice we gained the freedom to do things differently and to move closer to who we were naturally. As we connected more with our compassion, our retreats became filled with conversation about how we must sustain our planet, the planet that nourishes us, our Mother Earth, if we and all other life on it are to survive.

Healthy systems promote awareness of their internal interconnectivity through regular communication among their participants. This communication provides knowledge for necessary growth, repair, evolution, or even release. Without this feedback, stagnation can set in, causing waste to build up and areas to decay. Moving toward greater diversity, yet consistent with itself, life emerges in patterns. By guiding according to these organic principles and fostering and supporting the connections, leaders can help organizations develop in healthier and more sustainable ways.

In short, through our discussions together, we have come to realize that our understanding of spirituality adds another layer of connection within the Earthview. As we have defined, the spirit is a life-giving energy that connects us all; consequently, even beyond physical reciprocity, we share a spiritual relationship with all other beings on Earth. Just as this reality can serve to feed itself and deepen your sense of spirituality, we realize that spirituality itself "multiplies even as it is divided" (Kurtz & Ketcham, 2002, p. 33). We consider spirituality, therefore, a central component of the Earthview. We cannot disregard the spiritual nature of ourselves and of our environment and the integrity of the whole. All beings in life work together in a synergistic effort; truly, the whole is greater than the sum of its parts.

> *I truly believe that there is a huge difference between a manager and a leader. And it's really basic: In a command and control structure, you can assign a manager or a supervisor some power over what is being done. That's not a leader. A leader is not assigned; a leader is chosen. So, as an individual, you might decide that you want to lead; however, you won't be a leader until you look around you and find that there are people that have chosen you as a leader and to follow you. And choice is something very important to authentic leadership.*
>
> **(Interviewee)**

> *And what has been wonderful— I've been in this role with slightly different titles over time for five-going-on-six years, and the typical period of time is two to three (three really on the outside); and one of the reasons that I haven't burnt out on it yet is that I do feel that I have been very true to who I am. I think that is an important lesson.*
>
> **(Interviewee)**

It follows then that in healthy, integrated organizations, leadership must honor the need for connection and the reality of interdependency and approach boundaries of self and structure with flexibility and permeability. As effective leaders, we cannot separate who we are in one setting from who we are in the next. The fast-paced complexity and interconnections of the many roles we embody in our lives collectively require us to authentically "show up" in all that we undertake and accomplish. In fact, authenticity, what Delbecq (1999) describes as the integration of the "private life of spirit" and the "public life of work" (p. 346), generates strength and wisdom for leadership. This reality of holistic authenticity is actually one of the key resources that we can bring to and share with our organizations.

> *As a leader, you must be true to yourself and be honest with folks. That takes courage, but . . .*
>
> (Interviewee)

Although this seems so natural to most of us now, it actually represents a major departure from the way that women leaders thought and behaved in the past. Earlier work (Bailey & Neilsen, 1987) found that women executive directors of nonprofit organizations were reluctant (and usually silent) even among themselves to talk about what they really felt made for effective leadership. Much like the many transgendered, bisexual, and lesbian women who believed that their lives would be threatened if their sexual orientation and identities were to become public, the ideologies, perspectives, and practices of these women leaders remained removed from their workplaces. Yet, the interconnectivity of life informs our leadership, and our leadership, in turn, shapes our lives and our world. With the stakes of accountability so high, we have a tremendous responsibility to bring our whole selves to everything we do.

Cross-Trainings for the Soul

READINGS

▣ The works by Margaret Wheatley (1999), particularly one of her earlier books, *Leadership and the New Science: Discovering Order in a Chaotic World* (1999), connect leadership with the theories of quantum physics to help make sense of and sort through the various difficulties that arise in organizations. She also offers theories and suggestions for working with the "flow" in an organization to maximize capacity. At her Web site, http://www.margaretwheatley.com, you can find numerous articles on leadership and the challenges facing today's leaders.

▣ Diane Dreher uses Taoist wisdom in the everyday life situations that women face. *The Tao of Inner Peace* (1990) is superb for reflection and conversation. She has written several books that use Taoist wisdom as a base for the content.

▣ Be on the lookout for the 2008 publication by George Vaillant, *Spiritual Evolution*.

▣ Even though he looks at the impact of nature on children, Richard Louv, a Southern Californian journalist whose work with others has started the "leave no child inside" movement, offers wisdom for us all. He has authored *Last Child in the Woods* (2005). What is good for children is great for us as women leaders! Consult http://www.cnaturenet.org.

REFLECTIONS

▣ What aspects of your leadership style are most compatible with the Earthview? What attitudes and behaviors are most conducive to supporting relationship and participation?

▣ Reflect on our interconnections—locally, globally, and with nature. What conditions and circumstances have affected you in ways you could not foresee? What actions of yours have had farther reaching impacts than you anticipated? How might you leverage our interconnection for more positive benefits?

RHYTHMS & RITUALS

▣ Take time to be with nature. Even though you can now find pure oxygen in the stores, resist. Walk through a park on the way to work, or spend time outside at the beginning or end of the day, mindfully breathing in fresh air. It is important for each person to connect with Earth and be grateful for the blessings received. Our disconnect with Earth is often pretty thorough, especially if we are in urban areas. Create a garden, or even attend to a plant in your office. Small urban gardens can be created in unused areas that do not have to take up much space. Plants help replenish our air, and having green around you in some form is very important for remembering and reflecting on Earth principles that sustain all.

▣ Practice yoga or Pilates, which are especially good for keeping your spirit and body flexible. There are classes for these and other body-mind-spirit exercises to be found in most areas. You can check the Web or look in the phone book to find places close to you that will fit with your schedule.

PART TWO

Organizational Toxicity and Toxin Handlers

In those years, people will say, we lost track / of the meaning of we, of you /
we found ourselves / reduced to I / and the whole thing became /
silly, ironic, terrible . . .

—Adrienne Rich, "In Those Years," *Dark Fields of the Republic: Poems 1991–1995*

Not all organizations are unhealthy, but many are, especially for women. Despite the increasing number of women in leadership, we still fight the battles of our foremothers, working in systems that continue to be dominated by a culture of power for some and control over the others. Many organizations maintain their structures in alignment with the Western worldview. In these systems, individualism and autonomy are highly prized, hierarchies prevail, and competition is inherent. We celebrate people being the best more often than we celebrate our organizations functioning at their best.

As we explored earlier, the characteristics of the Earthview perspective, philosophy, and practices—interconnection, nurturing, engagement, cooperation, and partnerships— are often evidenced in women's approaches to leadership (Funk, 2004; Hackney &

All organizations and systems have unhealthy things within them. Like most women in the workforce, we have experienced a culture created by the fact that, in most societies, men have acceptance as leaders. Therefore, they act like leaders, and people follow them. Some are wonderful. Some are not. Some have been my partners along the way and have helped me become a competent and hopefully visionary leader. But it's hard, really hard. Some days it's not worth it. Sometimes you have to push so hard just to be accepted that you get bone tired. And as Fannie Lou Hamer once said, some days you get 'sick and tired of being sick and tired.'

(Retreat participant)

> *I have worked hard to get rid of my immediate response to anger and channel it into something construc- tive . . . I have also gone into the 'belly of the beast'. I was the presi- dent of my class from third grade through college. But then, after all the battering, I decided I was never going to represent the status quo again. So I switched to civil rights, women's rights, and other issues.*
>
> **(Interviewee)**

Runnestrand, 2003; Harris, Smith, & Hale, 2002; Hudson & Williamson, 2002; Ketelle, 1997). Women who lead tend to value rapport and the ability to build, support, and work through interpersonal affiliations (cf. Hudson & Williamson, 2002; Rosener, 1990). Even though many of these traits are now touted in the leader- ship literature as desirable for leaders regardless of gender, and even though we fundamentally know that they support us in our successes as women leaders, we still seem to struggle against the status quo to implement them effectively in our organizations.

Despite the degree to which leaders espouse the importance of inclusion and power sharing, these behaviors are not yet the norm in our institutions. Separation by department, unit, or division continues to be more common than connection. Fear still pervades much decision making. Attempts in good faith to flatten organizational structures have not yet yielded concomitant increases in organizational participation and involvement. Neither has the engagement of more women in leadership positions been sufficient to foster more open and creative organizations where people can thrive.

The conflict between what we need from our work environments and what we receive creates organizational dissonance for many women in leadership. This dissonance con- tributes to organizational toxicity. Toxicity is not to be confused with resistance. Resistance is a functional dynamic characteristic of healthy organizations. It is the man- ifestation of the natural tension that occurs as we learn and grow. It is an inherent ele- ment of change; it encourages us to work hard, achieve goals, and innovate. Toxicity, on the other hand, is different. In his book, *Toxic Emotions at Work: How Compassionate Managers Handle Pain and Conflict,* Peter Frost (2003) explored the dangers to leaders when toxic emotions accumulate in the workplace. He defined organizational toxicity as "the outcome of emotionally insensitive attitudes and actions of managers and the practices of their companies . . . [that act] as a noxious substance, draining vitality from individuals and your entire organization" (p. 13). It can manifest in many ways includ- ing the inability to trust, feelings of being out of control, resistance to change, and even physical illness (Porter-O'Grady & Malloch, 2007).

Toxicity is present to some extent in all organizations and perpetuated to varying de- grees by all leaders, sometimes simply as a consequence of the act of leading. As leaders and members of our organizations, we can propogate it or help to ameliorate it. If left unman- aged, increasing levels of toxicity significantly disrupt innovative and productive work.

Toxicity can be introduced into an organizational system from the outside or within. An unflattering portrayal of your organization in the media, a reduction in your bond rating, a change in service reimbursement rates from third-party payers, and a client's election to take his/her business elsewhere—these are all ways in which toxicity can enter a system from the outside. These are also organizational challenges that unify the organization by bringing colleagues together in an attempt to overcome them, in part because these challenges are public and are consciously recognized as having the poten- tial to damage the organization's viability if they are not appropriately managed. It is the attention given to these issues, often in the form of solidarity, that helps mitigate some of their negative impacts, if not practically, at least at an energetic level within the organization.

Internally, an overbearing boss, a subversive co-worker, a missed deadline, a departmental restructuring, or a series of unfulfilled expectations, any of these has the capacity to promote or exacerbate the development of organizational toxicity. These are also the challenges that tend to be ignored or, worse, punished within the organization. The suffering and emotional pressures employees face in their personal lives do not diminish as they walk through the office doors. They carry these stresses with them, and internal toxicity can interfere with how they perform in their work environments. Unfortunately, there are many wounded people in our organizations, people who are often unaware of their condition and its effects on themselves and others. Our internal conflicts can cause toxicity to accumulate; if we let these conflicts take over, we become oblivious to our impacts or simply incapable of helping others feel they make a difference, are connected, and are valued and valuable. When these pressures affect employee teams, departments, and professional relationships, the poison becomes endemic.

I think what gets in the way is the sense of barriers, whether financial, people, communication, or leaders' thought barriers. You're always adjusting to take into account these challenges and barriers that are put in your way. It seems that I've always been in situations where I'm trying to work in a discipline or a project or something that may not be valued by society . . . and I always feel that I'm working against a wall—gender, discipline, race, ethnicity—but what I like to do is challenge whatever the system is in relation to those things and make them see the value in whatever I'm doing.

(Interviewee)

I worked in extremely high-profile, high-risk projects. And I spent six years commuting . . . I was working on mergers and acquisitions in the early 1990s. Very high risk—this is not exactly the trail for the meek at heart—very dog-eat-dog. And women, you could be extremely successful, but I have to say that I worked twice as hard to get that same level of validation. It's just a way of life. So, I did that, and I became *exhausted. I lost the love . . . That was a year and a half before Enron . . . I was very close to being promoted as partner and that was great—youngest and being female. When I found out, I went out and celebrated for a day and then came back, and said, 'Geez, this is not what I want to shoot for at all. I cannot see myself aligning with the values of where this industry is going at all. So, therefore, I'm going to go.'*

(Interviewee)

Losing Heart

Women leaders cannot deny the feelings of alienation and struggle that often accompany leadership. Heifetz and Linsky (2002) talk about "losing heart." They describe how "your life juice (creativity, daring, curiosity, eagerness to question, compassion and love for people) can seep away daily as you get beat up, put down or silenced" (p. 225). When we take into account our multifaceted roles and the complexities of the organizational environments in which we serve, the link between losing heart and organizational toxicity emerges as part of a cycle. A system's toxicity can push us in the direction of unconstructive behaviors and emotions. As we try to defend ourselves in the face of the negative energy we are experiencing in toxic organizations, we are apt to manifest the very behaviors that characterize a loss of heart. We consequently weaken our connections with the life forces that sustain us, "turn[ing] innocence into cynicism, curiosity into arrogance and compassion into callousness" (Heifetz & Linksy, 2002, p. 226).

Let's consider a few scenarios that are all too common in our organizations. We may avoid certain people because they seem to find the fault in ideas rather than the possibilities. We may react in frustration when others feel stifled and constrained by inflexible regulations and excessive paperwork. We may decide not to give input in a meeting, maybe because we do not think it matters. We may be just overtired or burnt out. Maybe you have found yourself in one or more of these situations. If so, you are not alone. These are simple examples of how we often lose heart. The ramifications of our actions in these situations erode the relationships and positive core that support the health of our organizations. Our loss of heart is contagious, having potentially deleterious effects on the work environment and others in it. Pervasive and insidious, loss of heart can constrain the hope that helps us lead, the hope that engages others.

> *Don't be afraid to make mistakes. We tend to get wrapped around the axle of perfection. We are not perfect, we are people. We are going to make mistakes, and as long as we don't hurt someone or damage ourselves in some way, it's okay: We're going to recover. And what better way to learn a lesson than to make a mistake at it.*
>
> **(Interviewee)**

Fear: A Supertoxin

Fear is often the glue that holds toxicity in our organizations. It functions as one of the blocks to our wholeness. It keeps us frozen and, at best, stifles creative thought and new vision. Fear often forms the basis for systemic toxicity, revealing itself in many ways: rigidity, false acceptance and conformity, bullying and blaming, sexual harassment, lack of balance, unrealistic expectations, focus on scarcity, pain and suffering, dysfunction, and paralysis. These manifestations of fear are pollutants in our organizations and communities, just as pesticides and other chemicals are pollutants in our air, water, and soil. Too much pollution in our systems becomes toxic. It not only endangers our organizations, but it also endangers our leaders.

Throughout the *Sustaining Our Spirits* project, we talked often of fear—fear inherent in our organizations and ourselves. In this era that began on a large scale within the

United States with the tragic events of 9/11 and the destruction of the World Trade Center towers in New York City, the attack on the Pentagon, and the heroic crash of United Airlines Flight 93 in Pennsylvania, terrorism has become a much more commonly used term in the American lexicon. This word, with all its connotations, has fear at its foundation, and we live with it daily. Sometimes it is conscious and at the surface of our interactions; sometimes it is so deep within us that we do not even recognize it until it erupts into clear physical or emotional pain.

On a political level, fear has translated itself into a war against terrorism, creating a climate of violence that, once unleashed, has effects on every strata of our existence. In this climate, we find that many of our institutions have become more reactionary and defensive, closing out creative, innovative plans for renewal and often leading us to begin to question our beliefs and styles of leadership, our talents and abilities. Fear becomes an effective way of maintaining the status quo and forcing decisions that are not based on the recognition of connection and interdependence but rather are framed as survival or clinging to survival.

Where a culture of fear and anxiety is present, new limits are put on concepts such as democracy, freedom, and leadership. Many beliefs we once held need to be reexamined. Expectations change for leaders when the fear and anxiety pervasive in the culture lead to an operational ethos of scarcity over abundance. Missions can flounder. An understanding of resources that is limited to financial capital alone prevails, creating a climate that leads to control and restraint, where imagination is stilted and entrepreneurial risk taking is discouraged and even punished. On the other hand, when the focus is broadened beyond the bottom line, fruitful collaboration can take place.

In one of our interviews, a leading political consultant revealed her realization that creating partnerships among unlikely partners generates an atmosphere of creativity and even fun. One of her recent legislative proposals was a bill to create individual development accounts that would raise three dollars for every dollar that an individual contributed to these savings plans. The designated purpose of these accounts was to promote asset building among people with low incomes. They could use their savings to buy a house, go to school, or start a small business. Beyond the financial component, this up-and-out-of-poverty strategy brought together the banking community, credit unions, Native American tribes, and other community and economic development associations in the spirit of partnership around important issues and outcomes that would benefit many. The banks would waive services charges and minimum balances on these accounts so people with economic challenges could begin saving in small increments without incurring the traditional costs associated with lower balance accounts. In exchange, the banks would get Community Reinvestment Act credits, and they would have more customers and more accounts. Funders and donors would provide matching dollars and support economic development efforts in their community. The local university would teach financial literacy classes, utilizing their expertise and strengthening their credibility in the community by sharing their resources. Although not all community members agreed with this process, through this woman's leadership, ethical and transparent communication was promoted to overcome fears, producing a partnership that offered a broad range of benefits for many.

Toxin Handlers as Organizational Healers

Just as toxicity resides within our organizations, so, too, do people who are skilled at lessening or transforming its impacts on the system. A key to an organization's health in the face of poisonous energies is the effectiveness of its "'toxin handlers'—leaders who deal with something as potentially volatile as emotional pain in the workplace" (Frost, 2003, p. 4). Toxin handlers recognize pain and potentially damaging situations within an organization and act effectively to reduce or remove the toxicity. They hold perilous roles in their organizations, leaving themselves open to the direct effects of the poisonous emotions they are trying to abate in much the same way as people who handle physical toxins.

Look around. Every day, everywhere in the world, we face choices about our individual health, our families' health, our global health. When illness and tragedy strike, people intercede to ease each others' pain. Organizations operate in much the same way. We are all aware that there are members of our organizations who are charged with attending to the company's fiscal health. What we often do not consider is that there are also members of our organizations who help to preserve its greater well-being by focusing on the health, energies, and relationships of its people.

We all have different styles, needs, passions, and dreams. Even as women, we do not feel or lead the same ways. In the workplace, what others expect of us and what we expect of ourselves can have wide-ranging effects. Expectations have the potential to generate negative energies that can cause pain and ultimately damage the health of our organizations. At the same time, they can work for good. Acts of compassion and nurturing can dissipate negative energies, transforming them into positive forces.

Some people are better than others at recognizing personal and organizational stresses and finding ways to manage them productively. They are our organizations' healers. The essence of this role is to alleviate and, where possible, prevent "pain that strips people of their self-esteem and that disconnects them from their work" (Stark, 2003, p. 1). They are empathetic, compassionate individuals who respond to others' pain and find ways to ease it before it becomes contagious. Consider the people others gravitate to in times of crisis and the people in the cubicles and offices where others seem to regularly flow "just to talk"; their deep listening skills can be a key to dissipating toxic emotions and preventing the spread of negative organizational energies. These organizational healers are able to transform potentially destructive elements into support for growth and renewal.

As mentioned earlier, Peter Frost and his colleagues conducted considerable research on the development and handling of organizational toxicity; and while this research has shown that gender was not a determining factor in identifying toxin handlers, quite often, however, women are viewed as embodying these traits in the workplace, more so than men. In fact, research by Taylor et al. (2000) indicates that while the well-known fight-or-flight mode characterizes the primary physiological responses to stress for both men and women, the female response is nuanced with a pattern of tend-and-befriend; wherein tending involves protective, caring behaviors to reduce stress, and befriending entails the development of social networks of support. This seemingly makes women more adapted to the role of toxin handler, but it also leaves them more susceptible to organizational toxicity and its impacts (Frost, 2003). Our organizations need to be healed, and we, as women, can play a vital role. To do so, we must remain purposeful and aware of ourselves and others.

Before we explore the four primary toxic challenges to women's leadership, we would like to share some success stories. Our interviews and retreats revealed numerous examples of ways in which women leaders are promoting essential healing. The following story of one woman leader illustrates how:

An executive in a large, multinational corporation, this senior industry leader would generally experience two things when she walked into a room: First, the majority of the men who were in the business would approach and acknowledge the male colleague who was with her as a partner while ignoring her; and second, women from the organization would come up to her and give her a hug for no particular reason, regardless of whether they had met her previously or not. The reason for this reaction became apparent one day before a board meeting when she found another woman colleague nervously preparing for a presentation. She offered to help with the presentation and even sat down with her to prepare, page by page. After she had calmed the woman, she asked, "By the way, I've been having this thing happen for three years—I've been getting these hugs—I've never understood it; I would love to know why this is happening." And the woman completely changed her demeanor. Dropping her head, she said that most women simply do not feel that they fit in the industry, but they love what they do. When they see a woman executive come in, someone who has been successful and is driving the business, they have hope and believe that with continue hard work they can become like her.

Despite her prestigious position, this senior industry leader was experiencing firsthand the toxicity of discrimination in business. Yet without realizing it, her capacity to deal with it and succeed along with her support for others were mitigating the accumulation of this toxicity for others in the organization and the industry.

In our hierarchical organizations, the higher up a toxic "dump" occurs or is viewed to occur, the more likely it is to permeate the entire organization. The organizational impact of leaders who manage by exclusion, intimidation, and oppression can be insidious and deleterious throughout the system, much like the gender bias that permeated the industry described in the previous example. At the same time, the higher up in the organizational hierarchy a toxin handler is positioned, and the greater the number of connections she has, the greater the capacity for systemic healing. In the case of our colleague, her senior role and visibility within the corporation and the industry greatly expanded the impact of her actions.

A corporate leader highlighted the essence of toxin handling by creating a program for the women in her organization that would ultimately ameliorate some of the toxicity to which they were exposing each other. The need for the program was identified when she was approached by a male colleague after a major national meeting and was told that, although she was highly respected in the company for her major accomplishments, most of the female executives in the corporate offices did not support or even like her. This came as an incredible shock to her, especially because she had never met most of them before. Rather than turning to destructive personal or organizational behaviors, however, she turned her energies into something productive—a program that recognizes women through fostering dedication, connection, and sharing talents in order to respond to the needs of the greater world. Women throughout the organization are now participating, and they are experiencing positive results in terms of relationship building and mutual support.

Clearly, the nurturing styles of women, although not always overtly valued as organizational assets, may be of greater organizational value than many expect, helping to cleanse our organizations of toxicity before it reaches a dangerous level for the system as a whole. But what are the costs for the toxin handlers?

The stories that Frost (2003) recounts are almost identical to those shared in our retreats and interviews with other women leaders. Chronic sleeplessness, headaches, indigestion, heart palpitations, an inability to concentrate, and reoccurring colds and viruses were among the common symptoms. Tragically, more devastating physical and emotional illnesses were described as well. Ironically, although most of the women knew the research on the mind–body–stress connections (e.g., Kabat-Zinn, 1994; Naparstek, 1995; Selye, 1978), few of our women leaders had incorporated antitoxin behaviors into their daily lives. Despite our desires and commitments to caring for others, we are not as dedicated to caring for ourselves!

Many of our retreat discussions were laden with stories about the toxicity that we have faced as leaders and as women. When we reviewed these in combination with the experiences our women colleagues relayed in their interviews, we found they clustered around four main challenges: challenges to authenticity, challenges to work, challenges to balance, and challenges to self.

Challenges to Authenticity

Cultural and systemic barriers to women's leadership are among the most wide reaching. Despite the number of women in the workforce and the barriers that have been broken down by the leaders who have come before us, societal oppression, sexism, unrealistic expectations, and pressures to "play along" with traditional roles and power structures continue to challenge us daily. We still hear stories of women who hit Plexiglas ceilings; the ceilings bend some, giving the illusion of progress to women leaders, but they are very hard to break through.

A toxic challenge to women that plays into the Plexiglas phenomenon, one that we are still working to overcome, is stereotyping. Gender, racial, and ethnic stereotyping is discussed extensively in a variety of arenas—from research literature to popular literature, from team-building workshops to professional conferences. The stereotyping of women in leadership is particularly powerful, because it is more often than not accompanied by false expectations to be just like or even better than male colleagues and the oppression that is born out of fear.

As women, we are quite frequently our own worst enemies. Rather than creating strong supportive "old girls' networks," we often hold unrealistic expectations of other women leaders. In these situations, it becomes too easy for each of us to shirk our responsibilities as women, as colleagues, and as members of the same organizational family, so when things do not go as planned, we feel comforted in our ability to blame others, especially our leaders. We are not nurturing and encouraging when we persist in putting each other on pedestals. It is not only lonely on the pedestal, but it is also dangerous. The higher the pedestal, the more likely we are to get hurt when we fall. However, rather than helping to build the pedestal, if we instead focus our energy into surrounding each other with nets of caring and respect, our falls will be much safer.

A more subtle, but still real and demeaning, toxin is "microaggression" (Sue & Sue, 2007). The current research on microaggressions explores these acts from the perspective of race, but our retreats and interviews confirm that microaggressions can take place in the context of any difference. A microaggression is an act that, often unintentionally, emphasizes bias and difference among people and reinforces disparities in our organizations and institutions. In many cases, only the victims of the action realize it has occurred; this makes these acts more insidious and difficult to manage, because perpetrators and unknowing accomplices are prevented from acknowledging their complicity in creating psychological dilemmas for others. An example of a racial micro-aggression is the assumption that all Asians have strong mathematical skills. One may initially think that this assumption is not harmful, but it actually sets up false expectations, often adding pressure to the lives of the victims and creating tension in their relationships with people from other groups (Sue & Sue, 2007).

Women also experience microaggressions—from the expectation to have maternal instincts to assumptions about sexuality when women choose not to get married. Such microaggressions, not to mention blatant stereotypes, add to the toxicity of a workplace. Beyond our gender, there are so many invisible differences that contribute to our individuality; we can live and lead to our fullest only when these differences are respected and not glossed over or worse.

What sustains me is being around people who are willing to get to know you before boxing you. Stereotypes are still prevalent in this country.

(Interviewee)

Although many of the "-isms" are indeed dangerous, *multiculturalism* is a good "-ism" that can actually overcome microaggressions and enhance our organizations. Distinct from *diversity,* which focuses largely on the differences between and among people, multiculturalism refers to the reality of many cultures within many cultures—the divergent and similar ways in which we process information and generate new ideas and form opinions, as well as the acknowledgement of our many identities, the visible and largely invisible ways that we show up in life, including race, ethnicity, and culture of origin; gender, identity, and sexual orientation; intellectual, emotional, and physical abilities; faith, religion, and spirituality; language, dialect, and accent; socioeconomic class; political positions, and ideological perspectives. As leaders, we must choose to embody an "us and we" not a "we and them" approach to life. And we must acknowledge and honor our own multicultural nature.

We need to make choices that resonate with who we are as individuals, who we were created to be, and what we're really, really passionate about, instead of choosing to do things because we may feel pressure from other people to do things, or it's more socially acceptable to do them.

(Interviewee)

External stereotypes also support depersonalization within the workplace. In the reality-based movie, *The Devil Wears Prada,* the dreaded office boss Miranda calls all of her assistants "Emily" rather than by their real names. The cutthroat, competitive environment is a breeding place for fear and loneliness, and a healthy community fails to form. Our retreats and interviews made very clear that there are severe dangers to the leader as well as to the associates when they are trying to survive in nonsustainable habitats. In the workplace, one of the most difficult tasks for a leader is to be able to balance relationships in such a way that her unconscious mind-set does not break down rather than build up her colleagues. Years of hierarchical leadership structures have conditioned many of us to construct walls of separation that attempt to distinguish us from our colleagues, sometimes at everyone's expense.

Well, you're in a meeting, and you're sitting there with all executive males except for one other woman. And you're trying to land a point, and they're not hearing you or they're challenging you, and for her to raise her hand and say, 'You know guys, you're not hearing what [she] is saying! And what she is communicating to you will solve three of the biggest issues impacting the company right now—can you just listen to her?' Wow! It's amazing. Typically, we all just sat and didn't say anything, and we wonder why she doesn't get anywhere . . . and the guys don't do that! They're backing each other up every free moment.

(Interviewee)

Even though some environments have opened up to women's presence and voices in leadership positions, many still stifle our ability to speak truths and have them heard. Indeed, such oppressive environments can actually give way to physical manifestations of "voicelessness," as experienced by one women leader in our group who suffered from stress-related throat problems, which literally prevented her from speaking. As women leaders, it is our responsibility to change these conditions. It is rarely easy, but it can benefit everyone when we try.

Recognition is often cited in office surveys about how people want to be acknowledged or rewarded. Countering Miranda's example in *The Devil Wears Prada*, to know someone's name and use it is key in forming a workplace that not only is safe but also creates a culture in which all can thrive. Authentic interaction develops in settings where each person is treated as the subject of her own life. We may not like everyone with whom we work, but we can respect them for the gifts they bring, and everyone brings some kind of gift. In fact, as leaders, it is our responsibility to construct opportunities for everybody to bring at least most of their talents to their jobs; as individuals within a community, it is our duty to bring our gifts fully to the table, to share ourselves with others. Indeed, we impoverish the world if we don't!

Challenges to Work

In addition to the greater societal pressures, women leaders face challenges of the daily grind, just as all people do, which can contribute to the accumulation of stress. Many times, these challenges are actually good things; problem solving is part of any organization, and it forces leaders to think creatively and continue to learn to bring about something new and better. These sorts of challenges can actually be sustaining; they keep work and life new and exciting, giving way to accomplishment. At the same time, other legitimate, more difficult challenges also exist, which add to the level of toxicity with which leaders must contend.

Sometimes, one has to negotiate through personality conflicts, which can hamper respect and clear communication. Interpersonal relationships may be toxic, including those with people who report to the leader, the leader's colleagues, and even the leader's boss. A leader actually may find herself taking the fall for her boss's huge missteps! More generally, however, the conflicts are less severe. Different people may also bring different agendas, both healthful and unhealthful, to the table. Sometimes, these conflicting agendas simply require time and effort to unravel confusion; other times, the issues are more deeply rooted and serious, requiring much energy to deal with opposition. To move an organization forward, its employees must all be working toward the same goal; they must embrace the vision and mission. Although the multiple backgrounds and perspectives that each person can contribute are valuable, the variety paradoxically can pose a challenge to healthful and united action. Leaders must constantly be sensitive to the differences and understand when and how to adjust their thoughts and actions to take into account these challenges.

Decision making in general can be stressful. Leaders often have to make decisions that affect many people quickly and with limited information; and many times, there is no clear-cut solution. They have to choose from among many options, all of which may have some merit. Leaders must be constant learners who think broadly.

Challenges to Balance

Negotiating through the unpredictability as a woman leader is challenging. Often, it is difficult to be acknowledged and be accepted as leaders. We, as women leaders, know and have experienced that when we reach certain positions, we can be marginalized and assailed by those around us. We know that being strong and decisive has consequences. We also know that it is easy but dangerous to allow our work to consume our identity. We know too that even though we have the capacity of octopus women, we sometimes lose our balance. Our main goal is to determine how to regain it and to find ways to sustain it.

It has often been said that how you deal with tough times really defines your character, especially if you are in a leadership position in any organization. Smith and Ross (1999) describe how this may be so:

> In golf there is plenty of time to reflect on your previous performance and plan your next shot . . . But leading an organization is more like polo. The little white ball no longer waits for you. It's always in motion. You no longer stand on firm ground; you carry a mallet and ride a galloping horse. Your teammates are also mounted on horses; and you have to coordinate your actions with them. Your opponents surround you, moving at fast speeds, intent on knocking the ball away. Horse manure flies everywhere. And the coach remains far away from you, shouting advice from the sidelines that you probably can't hear. (p. 110)

Although none of us ever played polo, this description vividly resonated with our experiences and stories from others about the lives of women leaders. Within organizations, women often play the roles of cleanser, purifier, and, as we said earlier, healer. As a matter of course, we filter information and resources, manage conflict, and mitigate challenges in the workplace. As we daily make critical decisions, sometimes with minimal information and with even less time for reflection, our required actions have us looking exactly like polo players!

Furthermore, women are called to take upon many roles outside of work, which men often do not attend to in the same capacity, such as child care, home life, volunteering, and so on. Indeed, all of these aspects are important, but they may sometimes distract us from setting high standards and professional goals. Added to these distractions is the pressure for women to fulfill their quota of, as one interviewee described it, "women stuff."

With all of these competing goals, women leaders can easily fall prey to burnout. Long hours at work can lead to physical, mental, and emotional exhaustion, especially in an unsupportive work atmosphere. The additional demands outside of work add another dimension of life to balance. Most organizations still demand rigid work hours and fail to offer flexible policies that help accommodate the reality of employees' caretaker roles outside of work. This can sometimes cause women leaders to make difficult and painful choices regarding their ability to remain in the workforce.

Interpersonal relations at work can also challenge a sense of balance. Clearly, it is important to enjoy collegial, positive relationships at work; these not only make daily interactions pleasant but also foster productive teamwork. We might take a step further to say that if we are truly able to adopt the Earthview perspective and appreciate life's interconnections, we would understand that each individual brings a personal dimension of self to work, which we, as leaders, must acknowledge. At the same time, we can experience the challenge of balancing the personal and professional nature of our relationships with our colleagues. Indeed, it is important to care for our colleagues, yet we must be able to balance this care without compromising the professional goals and work that must be accomplished. This demands psychological maturity and transparency from both us and our co-workers to clarify how we can handle our relationships so that they can continue to work and move forward.

> *I'm in this situation right now where my closest friend is a board member. We had that conversation. She's a fabulous leader in the community, as am I, and we said that we're not going to talk about the public aspect of our work . . . Transparency is the best thing in a delicate situation. Everything is fine when people know how we're handling it. We don't talk about personalities and work. It's been tricky, but it has functioned. We've figured out the best thing for the organization and for each of us personally. And then we've disclosed that.*
>
> **(Interviewee)**

Challenges to Self

Many women leaders, like those in the *Sustaining Our Spirits* group, have sought ways to manage their challenges and struggles and to sustain the original fire of compassion that brought them to leadership. Unfortunately, this searching can sometimes also lead to loneliness—a loneliness that arises out of deep-seated questions, causing us to wonder whom we can trust and what the implications for our leadership will be if we dare show weakness. Research by Boyatzis and McKee (2005) has recognized that the loneliness that comes from being the leader is a major component of "power stress," which over time leads us to sacrificing ourselves to chronic stress. Sometimes this stress becomes so overwhelming that it can lead to actual violence; accounts of women leaders' tragic suicides are all too familiar to us. Boyatzis and McKee (2005) contend that to manage "the cycle of sacrifice and renewal" and actually maintain "resonance," leaders must "understand that renewing oneself is a holistic process that involves the mind, body, heart, and spirit" (p. 8).

Because we have yet to come to a true partnership model of leadership, we continue to ignore the Earthview and function within a hierarchical paradigm that equates separate with good and in which the illusion of control is rewarded. Not only do we seal off the dysfunctional units of our organizations instead of attending to them, but we also isolate ourselves from the very people and practices that sustain us, and we increase the threats to our existence. Both organizationally and personally, when we operate from the "separate is better" worldview or are forced to operate in this way, we find ourselves in conflict with ourselves. It is then that physical symptoms occur in our bodies as a way of reminding us of our internal disconnect. It is imperative that as women we begin to recognize and heed the things our bodies tell us.

As we delved into our discussions, each one of us shared instances when we felt alone and vulnerable in our leadership roles. We realized, somewhat paradoxically, that our feelings of loneliness do not signify that we are actually alone. Despite it all, we still are connected, and we cannot withdraw ourselves from others absolutely, risking further damage, for as Heifitz and Linksy (2002) state, "Leadership takes the capacity to stomach hostility so you can stay connected to the people, lest you disengage from them and exacerbate the danger" (p. 18). The danger of disconnecting from those with whom you lead and work means that you become less able to do both—lead and work—often triggering a disintegration of morale and leading colleagues to form various factions instead of gathering with you in support. Yet, creating a culture in which community can thrive is not a simple process. Our interconnection—the relationships we share and the ways in which we make an impact on one another—is often not accessible to our consciousness.

We know that violence and breakdown begin first in our minds (Nagler, 2001). The images of harmful propaganda have touched the minds and hearts of people, planting the seeds of jealousy, anger, and disdain that objectify others, ultimately leading to war. How simple it is to discount an individual who does not fit within our frame of reference.

> *The name of the game is to 'suck it up' . . . and then it comes out in physical symptoms.*
>
> **(Retreat participant)**

> *As leaders, we often feel disconnected and lonely. We worry about rejection and failure. We strive to do our best in all aspects of our lives— as leaders, as partners, as mothers, as daughters. We try to do it all. It's no wonder that we get tired. Our bodies incorporate the stress, and we feel the strain . . . My husband says it's no wonder I have rotator cuff injuries . . . I am carrying the world on my shoulders. After years of pushing, your back doesn't work. After years of carrying the world, your shoulders freeze.*
>
> **(Retreat participant)**

> *How are we going to lead in the future? Will we fall into the same traps as men have? It is so dangerous to just plug into the system.*
>
> **(Interviewee)**

Furthermore, many women face a myriad of degrading pressures. Mass acceptance of elective surgery to alter body parts—from to eyelids, to breasts, tummies, and even knees—propagates a perverted and superficial role for women in society. In some ways, women's rights have become dissipated and distorted in such a way that sexual behaviors and body reshaping have become more identified with the freedom we are seeking than our ability to contribute our wisdom to reshaping society, a society that currently seems to value consumerism and denial over justice and compassion.

Perhaps like the canary in the mine, women are sensitive to the culture of fear and violence that continues to build in our organizations and around the world. The old questions and doubts surface: Am I good enough? Am I smart enough? Will I be successful enough? They gnaw at us even as we thought or hoped that, having reached the status of leaders, we were far from these worries. Women leaders feel pressure to "do it all." Even though external pressure surely exists, we also must face the fact that we often place internal pressure on ourselves. We are not "superwomen," and working longer and harder will not help us. We can strive to work smarter, to be better every day, but carrying expectations about perfection with us only undermines our self-esteem and our journey.

> We tend to wear more hats than our male counterparts. We are expected to be more to more people than our male counterparts, and so we have to divide our time more than we would like to amongst different constituencies.
>
> **(Interviewee)**

This challenge brings us full circle—back to the initial challenge of authenticity and false expectations. When we become disconnected from ourselves, we become disconnected from others. We are just as likely to create the pedestals from which we might fall as our colleagues. To fall from a pedestal, regardless of whether it was created for us by our own expectations or by those of others, is to fall much harder than when we are standing on the ground, centered by our own awareness, and side by side with our colleagues, friends, and families. When we acknowledge and embrace our uniqueness and the reality of our connections, we are leading with the power of the whole, and there are more people to steady us if we falter.

Leadership–Toxicity Paradox

The organizational environments in which we are striving to excel threaten our very existence as leaders. How can we nurture and grow our organizations when they are unhealthy? And how can we nurture and grow ourselves amidst this toxicity? This fundamental challenge was at the center of the *Sustaining Our Spirits* project. Patterns of behavior learned over time influence individual and organizational action, and these patterns, shaped by traditional organizational models, challenge the sustainability of women as leaders.

> Don't be afraid to take risks. Don't be afraid to fail.
>
> **(Interviewee)**

We can accept that organizations carry toxicity within them and that there are responsive and compassionate people within organizations that can assist in the healing process. The larger question is how do we help our organizations become even stronger, even healthier, even better? In part, it is a matter of prevention. Environmental protectionists have long known that it is far more efficient and productive to stop toxic waste from entering our natural habitats than it is to remove it once it is there. Could adopting a different worldview actually improve the health of our organizations by reducing the amount of toxic energy that enters them? If we understood and regularly put into practice Earthview principles, would that make the difference in leading and working in our healthy organizations and systems?

Earth, as a system, has its own way of rebalancing toxicity. Earth continually creates; as Swimme and Berry write (1992), there is a "creative process whence the universe derives, sustains itself, and continues its sequence of transformations" (p. 251). This cosmic view may be too grand to contemplate when we consider the role of toxic organizations, but if all truly is one, we are part of the problem, the dilemma, and the resolution.

Organizational conventions evolve, but they do so in a manner that seeks to maintain equilibrium. Sometimes a more radical approach is needed to achieve the changes we seek. A forest fire is devastating in its violence, yet it offers a stunning example of how powerful the forces of change are and how massive disruptions can ultimately lead to rebirth. Changing the organizational landscape may require a similar series of events. The tension created for leaders seeking to challenge the organizational balance can lead initially to a higher degree of ambiguity and dysfunction for the organization and a heightened sense of personal anxiety and powerlessness. A leader's customary response to this sense of flux is a move to establish greater control, pulling in or centralizing power. Yet this only perpetuates ingrained organizational patterns and hinders opportunities for real transformation.

In our natural systems, some things must be pruned or even die to support growth and renewal. In much the same way, many conventional, organizational standards and mores must give way to new ideas. Some, like most plants, can be contained and, with a little extra care, prevented from overrunning newly germinating ideas. Others can be toxic and, like invasive and poisonous species, can pose an even greater threat to an organization's wellbeing. These need to be permanently removed to support healthy growth, innovation, and change.

The process of minimizing and transforming organizational toxicity involves both death and regeneration. It can take time and can

> *An area of my gravest concern: when a project fails and others have believed in my leadership, I have let them down . . . personally. So many folks pin their hopes on my ability to succeed. I have failed them and that weight is the heaviest of all . . . I carry guilt. I carry remorse. I carry fear for their well being. And yet, I rise. Go figure.*
>
> **(Interviewee)**

> *Being a successful leader is less about what the barriers were than addressing and growing from potential failures. That's what becomes sustaining. It's about having the ability to deal with failure, grow from it, overcome it, and become a better leader.*
>
> **(Interviewee)**

> *What I find sustaining is the sense or feeling that on a day-to-day basis, you are making a difference, and you feel that. Either through the work that you do that day, the people you interact with, a decision that you've made that you feel good about . . . It's a sense of having some confirmation that you're making a difference. When you get to the point when you feel that you're not, that's when it's time to leave that role because otherwise, you won't be healthy for the organization.*
>
> **(Interviewee)**

> *Is there a responsibility that goes with leadership? The answer is yes . . . the next level of responsibility is action . . . and it is an expectation of action. I can be a model of peace and have peace in myself but if I stop there, I fall short of my full responsibility . . . Our leaders have gone so astray . . . If not me, who? If not now, when? The personal is not enough. There is a growing movement around the world of people starting to connect on issues like this.*
>
> **(Retreat participant)**

require the investment of considerable energy. Thus, at the heart of the leadership-toxicity paradox is a challenge for women leaders: We must be strong, healthy leaders in organizations that hold within them the realities of their own death and dying and the multiple opportunities for systemic poisoning and dysfunction.

A large international corporation recently discovered a sense of renewal through the birthing of innovative strategies. Specifically focused on appliance and technology equipment sales, the company originally targeted a male market; however, through the research of one of their woman leaders, it discovered that there were more women than men purchasing its products. To tailor the company's products and services to the female-dominated market, as well as enhance its own profits, this woman began an initiative to reinvent the organization. Reaching out among her community, she convened a group of woman executives who agreed to volunteer their time and energies around specific, focused projects that would help determine the direction that the organization could take. Not only has this project enhanced the corporation, but the participating women have built a network of relationships with others and have honed new skills.

As leaders, we are expected to be strong and healthy. At the same time, we are expected to cleanse our organizations of their systemic toxicity, to act as the filters for all the negativity, the challenges, and the fears within them. What can we, as leaders, do about these conflicting expectations? Each of the *Sustaining Our Spirits* partners struggled with this question in very personal and public ways during our time together. Through personal reflection and dialogue, some contemplated significant life and career changes, others sought ways to place greater emphasis on self-care, and still others worked to find ways to do more community building within their organizations. We each were at different stages of our journeys, and we made our own choices bolstered by the support of the other women who listened, understood, and helped us choose the best ways for ourselves.

This is where spirit comes in again. We know that love and compassion can overcome fear. By open-heartedly joining with each other as leaders and as women, we can share the information that we have. With one another, we can discover new ways to break the grip of fear and toxins that hold us captive. As we heal ourselves, we can heal each other and lead our organizations and our world more positively into the future.

They are intriguing against one another—it's the same internalized oppression that presents barriers to women working with women. Women do not talk about or acknowledge this woundedness.

(Interviewee)

Cross-Trainings for the Soul

READINGS

- Peter Frost's foundational book *Toxic Emotions at Work: How Compassionate Managers Handle Pain and Conflict* (2003) offers incredibly valuable information about how to protect yourself and your organization in the face of toxicity.
- Ronald Heifetz has provided a valuable contribution to the leadership canon with his first book, *Leadership Without Easy Answers* (1994). This was followed by the collaborative book with Marty Linsky, *Leadership on the Line: Staying Alive Through the Dangers of Leading* (Heifetz & Linsky, 2002).
- Explore *Leading from Within* (2007) by Sam M. Intrator and Megan Scribner, a soothing and provocative collection of thoughts and experiences of leaders matched with their favorite poems.

REFLECTIONS

- Consider a variation on an inquiry posed by Jim Collins (2001) in *Good to Great*. Set aside some time and review your life. Then ask yourself whether you would still do what you are doing now if you felt financially secure for the next 30, 40, or 50 years, or if you knew that you had less than five years to live. Why did you respond to this query the way you did? What does your response mean in terms of appreciation and action?
- Explore your motivations and contributions. Why and how do you lead? What are some of the fundamental strengths you bring to this role? How have they been or how can they be valuable in promoting connection?

RHYTHMS & RITUALS

- Develop a meditation practice. Meditation can be used for cultivating greater self-awareness, centering, developing compassion and forgiveness, and overcoming fear. In addition to helping you incorporate individual time for deep reflection, meditation can be especially powerful in dealing with toxicity. There are many outstanding resources you can consult if these areas are new to you. Pema Chodron's books, including *The Places That Scare You* (2001) and *When Things Fall Apart* (1999), provide much wisdom. *Radical Acceptance* by Tara Brach (2003) outlines many guided meditations in areas that can strengthen your soul and enhance your leadership.
- Pay attention to your dreams. They can tell you a lot about issues you are facing. Pay attention to how you felt during the dream. What symbols do you remember? What information can you access from your unconscious by working with your dreams? Keeping a dream journal can be very helpful, especially if you are having vivid or disturbing dreams. Our unconscious can give us information about ourselves— symbols are particularly important in dreams. Seek resources for dream work, such as Jungian organizations in your particular location.

Self-Knowledge as a Foundation for Sustenance

Only when we are no longer afraid do we begin to live in every experience,
painful or joyous, to live in gratitude for every moment, to live abundantly.

—Attributed to Dorothy Thompson

To fully conceptualize how women in leadership sustain themselves, we needed to explore beyond our high points and inspirations. In addition to identifying aspects within our relationships—with fellow employees, services, products, clients, patients, and communities—that have made our work most meaningful, our inquiry led us to some of the buried places, the places we do not often acknowledge, even to ourselves. These are the deepest recesses of who we are as leaders. We understood that this was going to be a spiritual journey and that these journeys are about profound rememberings and shedding untruths. We had come to an understanding that we needed to go to that essential place to develop the hardiness and stamina required of us to do more. Like descending into a jagged mountain crevasse, simply reaching this place can be treacherous, yet it provides great potential for learning—learning about ourselves and learning with our fellow adventurers. This not only allows us to speak the truth about our lives but also to find the fortitude to do the job required of us, without which we would not have the resilience to move the fruits of those deep conversations to action.

> We . . . knew that if we didn't go deep, we wouldn't go anywhere. Staying on the surface wouldn't get us to that deep understanding of ourselves as leaders.
>
> **(Retreat participant)**

Once we quieted ourselves for evocative reflection and sharing about women and leadership, we found that we had to confront many powerful themes. Entrenched truths surfaced about which we rarely dare speak. Stories of illness, feelings of abuse, the sense of being misunderstood, pulled off balance, emotionally beat-up, and exhausted in our work, all of which spilled over into other parts of our lives, were more common and more damaging than many of us had thought. During this

We are 24-hour women, octopus women, doing eight things at once and we can also do a ninth—but there is a need for balance. You can lose it, but can you get it back?

(Retreat participant)

contemplation and dialogue, we realized that many of our personal dangers were linked directly to toxicities in our organizations and to the inherent fears that perpetuated them. As we wrestled with the leadership-toxicity paradox, our sharing revealed stories of physical pain and illness, personal attacks, and a search for wellness, balance, and self.

Together, we were able to listen to each story with open and empathetic hearts. As we individually began to recognize and then accept the deep impacts of our organizational disease, we began to better understand why certain events were more toxic for some than others.

One woman suddenly realized that her continued need for approval from her father actually made her most vulnerable to the indirectly expressed criticisms, annoyances, and disapproval from a more senior male colleague. Even though she was able to protect herself when her co-worker's anger was explicit, his covert nature of self-expression led her directly to feelings of being unprotected and "a disappointment."

We knew that we were not one another's therapist, but we began to appreciate the therapeutic quality of deep listening and dialogue. Our experiences resonated with the beautiful description offered by Lawrence-Lightfoot (1999) in her treatise on respect: "We [were] in a hall of mirrors, seeing ourselves reflected in each other's eyes, hearing our conversations echoed in their stories . . . [establishing] relationships that move[d] toward symmetry and intimacy" (p. 13). We became increasingly energized in the company of one another, and we drew new life from dynamic rituals and meditations on the wisdom of the Earth. We sought fresh insights, as we explored the challenges within the realities that we faced. We found a renewed sense of optimism as we focused on our questions of challenge and sustenance, individually and together, and we united around the importance of reaching balance and boundaries for ourselves and our organizations.

Through our exploration of that which gives us life and keeps us connected, we arrived at the understanding that, in a deeply spiritual way, we were each in search of ways to lead from our sense of self, our authenticity. In recounting his journey of self-discovery around work and life, David Whyte (2002) poetically described the transformative power of entering into your elemental waters and connecting with that to which you can give your whole self. His conversation with Brother David on this topic spoke directly to our own struggles with leadership:

> The antidote to exhaustion is *wholeheartedness* . . . You are so tired through and through because a good half of what you do here in this organization has nothing to do with your true powers, or the place you have reached in your life. You are only half there, and half here will kill you after a while. You need something to which you can give your full powers. You know what that is; I don't have to tell you. (pp. 132–133)

Wheatley (2005) talks about "attending to your personal spiritual health"; Heifetz and Linsky (2002) discuss "finding your sacred heart"; and Collins (2005) calls us to "level 5 leadership." Lesser (1999) reminds us that:

The soul will more readily come out of hiding if the incarnated self is loved. How will you know if you are nourishing your soul? Remember what Rumi says: 'When you do things from your soul, you feel a river moving in you, a joy.' (p. 337)

The wisdom in these messages is that going deep to connect with your life energy is essential for wholeness and vitality. It is not something we strive for in our personal lives to augment our leadership; it *is* our leadership.

BEING A WOMAN LEADER OF COLOR

I embody many differences—both visible and invisible. Visibly, I am a woman, and I am a woman of color; invisibly, among other things that make one unique, while I find emotional sustenance in both men and women, I have had a long-term partnership with a woman. In terms of the visible differences, I look forward to the day when I can walk into a room and the "men in suits" approach me and converse with me without making me feel like I need to showcase my credentials or have that done by a "handler." At the risk of generalizing, truly, men—especially those who are tall, white, and apparently heterosexual—command the room's attention when they enter. Although some things have changed over the years, women still do not receive the same reception; many times, it is assumed that we are the assistants or secretaries for a man.

Recently, I sat on a panel with two other female deans—both of whom are from different disciplines and have very different visible and invisible characteristics—and we discussed being a woman leader. One of the women, who happened to be white, said that she had never experienced differences as a woman leader. This shocked me! I immediately said that I had felt differences, both positive and negative. I suspect that being a woman of color might have been a factor for me, but I also know that "difference" is contextually based.

As I look back over my life, I realize that there have been times when I have been particularly conscious of certain differences. For example, during the 1960s and early 1970s, I was most aware of being a black woman; I felt very aware of my race and how it connected me to other African Americans. During the 1970s and 1980s, my gender felt more prominent, and in the 1990s to date, I have been keenly aware of both my gender and race. So, as the societal and cultural atmosphere has changed, the visibility of differences has shifted, and so have my alliances based on race or gender.

Differences bring both challenges and blessings. Some people have come right out and said that my identity is the "icing on the cake" of my skills. Others have sought alignment or even favors from me; whenever I am "the first" in my position, I always feel a great deal of expectation from the black community. When appointed as the first in an academic setting, for example, one young black male student even approached me by saying, "Hey, sistah! I'm going to get an 'A' now, right?" The gay-lesbian-bisexual-transgender community in all of my workplaces has also actively sought my attention.

A part of all of these communities, I feel a sense of pride, but also accountability and deep responsibility that together add another dimension to my work. As a "first" in many of my positions, I know that I have to "succeed"—I am clear that I do not want to be the "last."

Giving Voice

As we have intimated, sharing and giving voice to ourselves and to others is not easy. Much has been written on the topic of women's voices in the role of leadership, but actually understanding voice is very challenging. This became increasingly clear to us in our circle of women leaders. When we began our retreats in the summer of 2003, each woman brought with her not only her personality and individual issues but also a collective amount of "baggage" that she had unwittingly assumed under the aegis of her leadership role. Through our stories, we discovered the costs for speaking our truth, of taking the courageous stand with those who had a hard time "hearing" us. During these times, we remembered the need for deep compassion for ourselves and others.

The concepts of *voice* and of *women's voices being heard* were very popular in the feminist movement and its literature during the 1960s through the 1980s. Having a voice implies that a person can bear influence on a situation by sharing her thoughts and feelings, which can shape knowledge and future action to be taken. Feminist theory shows us how masculine, Western culture has sown seeds of oppression that hinder women from speaking out and being heard and understood. In their groundbreaking study, *Women's Ways of Knowing*, Belenky and colleagues (Belenky, Clinchy, Goldberger, & Tarule, 1986) show how women describe themselves, their knowledge, and their ability to act through the metaphors of *voice* and *silence*. Whereas visual images tend to imply distance and passivity, voice and silence portray a different kind of interaction with others: having something or nothing to say; (not) being part of a conversation; or being heard or being drowned out in the many voices, particularly male, in their lives. Many of the learning activities women tend to use, such as asking questions, listening to others, and refraining from speaking out, signal helplessness according to the Western model, which can cause women to doubt themselves and their abilities.

Voice for women leaders has often been a tenuous subject. Women who speak the "party line" have been more accepted than those who speak their own truths. Often in meetings, women's ideas are pushed aside or ignored or even repeated later by a male colleague. Sometimes, women are only perceived to be heard when they become angry or accusatory. In certain settings, this has been tantamount to career suicide; therefore, some women have kept silent. Rather than reverting to the extremes of silence on the one hand or constant pontificating at the other, we must seek a balance of reflection and articulation. Women's voices are most healthy and effective when they integrate both internal and external sources of knowledge to learn, create, and grow.

Cognitive research from Colwill (1995) shows that girls tend to begin speaking earlier than boys, produce longer and more complicated sentences, possess larger vocabularies, and make fewer grammatical errors in their conversation and writing. As they grow older, women are more likely to utilize communication styles that foster participation through self-disclosure, personal references, and emotions, whereas men tend to use informal and third-person pronouns, imperatives, slang, and aggressive language. Men also more frequently interrupt others and change topics. Furthermore, women are more likely to recover verbal capabilities after a stroke than men.

Colwill (1995) also found that women are often perceived as being less intelligent than men because in their communication they tend to use polite verbal forms more often than men; add tag questions to their statements; use disclaimers and qualifiers more frequently than men; and speak in a soft, breathy, high pitch that resembles a little girl. Men tend to talk about their accomplishments more readily than women, as well. It is interesting that the most effective leaders tailor their communicative styles by crossing over and adopting characteristics of the style of the opposite sex.

The ability to clearly communicate and express oneself is referenced, time and time again, as a key skill for leaders to possess. Indeed, understanding the concept of discourse, which helps people comprehend their positions in relationships to and with others, is a key focus of feminist thought (Grogan, 2002). Discourse, in fact, is contextual. Most environments have rules for discourse—cultural understandings about to whom, when, and how people speak together. Given the many realms in which we, as leaders, find ourselves, it is critical that we are aware of the appropriateness of the multiple forms of discourse in which we might engage.

> *So, time and time again, I've had to explain that on the one hand, my standards are extremely high, what we deliver out of our organization is of extremely high quality, and my standards for performance and what's acceptable and what's not acceptable are extremely high; I'm just not a jerk when I deliver the message.*
>
> (Interviewee)

LEARNING THE JOY OF JOURNALING

When I first became a Dean, I was so fortunate to have a woman come into my life who became my spiritual guide. It was more than the fact that she was a Roman Catholic nun. This woman had heard of my appointment and felt "called" to meet me. A W. K. Kellogg Leadership Fellowship enabled me to very modestly compensate her for her time and gasoline. Her steady and safe support provided me the space I needed to begin to tease apart some of the complexities inherent in the realities of my new leadership responsibilities. Our work together became a lived "Serenity Prayer," with her gentle guidance in discerning the differences among the situations in which I had the ability to control the process and outcome (very small in numbers), those circumstances in which I could determine the process and had to trust that the "right" outcome emerged (more of the time), and then most of those times where I could outline or suggest the process and then let go and trust those who were directly involved. I began to keep a journal, an accounting in my own words for "my eyes only," of all of these situations that allowed me to really see—to have the evidence—that entrusting talented colleagues led to better process and product outcomes.

More recently my partner bought me a blessings book, a small notebook for me to look beyond and beneath the issues I continue to face as a leader to record the often forgotten gifts that I receive, those moments of sheer joy that also come with my position of responsibility. This continues to be a wonder-full way to stop and acknowledge why I work as hard and as long as I do . . . and remember to say thank you.

One woman leader who has long been working in a male-dominated field is very aware of the different discourses that she encounters. While working at one institution, she developed a close friendship with a male colleague with whom she would attend meetings. After each meeting, she would make a point of connecting with him so that he could "translate" what had been said, both verbally and nonverbally by the other male colleagues, so that she could understand what had happened, in addition to what she had perceived had happened. Opportunities like this help people navigate through their careers and bridge the distance between disparate perspectives.

Awareness and acknowledgement of the different discourses that might be present can foster dialogue. By understanding that different perspectives and forms of communication exist, we can be most present and attentive to both our sharing of ourselves and our openness to others. As women leaders, we know how important it is for us to have a safe space to share our feelings, tensions, and anxieties; simply venting can be enough to refresh and re-center our spirits. Similarly, we must strive to ensure that the environments in which we lead offer a safe haven for dialogue in which everyone can risk both giving voice to their own stories and hearing those of others.

> *You have to be vulnerable enough to express yourself to others, and get out there to communicate and share ideas. Allow them to interact, observe, be involved with, and experience what that's like. Otherwise, it's all behind a curtain and you're not going to have as deep of a leadership and relationship.*
>
> **(Interviewee)**

Cross-Trainings for the Soul

READINGS

▪ John Heider looks at leadership from the perspective of the Tao. His book, *The Tao of Leadership: Leadership Strategies for a New Age,* was first published by Bantam Books in 1985. Applying the ancient wisdom of the Tao to leadership is supportive and insightful for all leaders, particularly for women leaders.

▪ Thich Nhat Hanh has many books from which to learn and meditate on the way of the peaceful leader in society, including *Anger: Wisdom for Cooling the Flames* (2004).

REFLECTIONS

▪ Reflect on your leadership. What have been some of your highpoints? Recall one or two experiences that make you especially proud. What made them so special? What was your role? How did this experience make you feel? How does reflecting on it make you feel now? You can also adapt this reflection by inquiring into your voice—those times when you had the courage to say what needed to be said or those times when you did not, and then change the ending by saying what needed to be said. Committing to this type of reflection regularly can help you amplify your voice as a woman and a leader.

▪ Consider the quote from David Whyte (2002) about wholeheartedness we cite on page 60. Explore it deeply in relation to your life. To what are you willing to give your full powers?

RHYTHMS & RITUALS

▪ Read poetry, write poetry, and/or keep a collection of favorite poems. This can be incorporated into your journaling. For example, create a Rumi journal. Jelaluddin Rumi was born in Balkh, Afghanistan, then part of the Persian Empire, in 1207, and his poetry offers a wealth of wisdom about leadership and self-awareness. His poetry and writings, along with more information on his life and work, can be found at http://www.rumi.org.uk, and have long been treasured by all who read them. Again, you might consider consulting *Leading from Within* (Intrator & Scribner, 2007), as a modern-day version.

▪ It may seem that you do not have enough time to read, but do it. Find a variety of books—not just work-related material. Good novels fill our imagination with other images and help us make larger connections with our world and others. Join a book club—just for fun—and share your thoughts with them. Look into books about other countries and places that you have never visited. Allow others to read to you; explore books on tape. This can open up whole new perspectives about your world.

CHAPTER SIX

Aligning Our Mission

*I always bear in mind that my mission is to leave behind me the kind
of impression that will make it easier for those who follow.*

—Attributed to Marian Anderson

L ike the diamonds in Indra's net described earlier, our search for wholeheartedness—the centeredness that allows us to be and bring our complete selves to life
and work—has countless facets and reveals many connections. Each aspect of our journey is its own, yet it is linked inextricably to all others. Each action and each choice are
independent, and in them, we see all the others we have made. As we exist in the present, we also embody our past and our future.

One of the most personal of our diamonds,
one that reaches to the depths of our souls and
one for which the existence and necessity of
interconnection is abundantly clear, is mission.
As we articulate our individual purposes, we are
not only describing what we want to achieve but
also expressing the essence of who we are. We
are claiming our internal passions and pursuing
them publicly in our personal and work lives.
The manifestation of our *raison d'être*—our reason for being—originates in the co-construction
of our lived experiences with others and the constant reintegration within ourselves.

> *Follow your dreams, if you have
> them. Don't let day-to-day realities
> get in the way of what you feel that
> you have been put here to do. We
> were all put here to do something
> special. Trying too hard to survive
> gets in the way.*
>
> **(Interviewee)**

Personal Mission

Effective leaders lead from vision and through mission. As noted by the "father of management," Peter Drucker (1992), "The first job of a leader is to think through and de-

fine the mission of the institution" (p. 3). We must pay attention to the talents and passions of those with whom we work and the needs and opportunities external to our organizations in order to focus our work optimally. It is critical for us, as leaders, to talk about missions and visions for our organizations, but we less frequently talk about how our personal visions and missions shape the way we lead; however, they affect not only how we lead but why, when, and for whom. When we successfully combine wholeheartedness with mission, we are able to coalesce our knowledge, skills, aspirations, and action; dig deeply into our own authenticity; and set the direction for a purpose-filled life in which we can thrive.

We are all called to leadership for different reasons. Our personal callings are relevant and important. Our first step is to define and understand what our personal missions are, to be cognizant of why we invest ourselves in what we do. This is critical. Because of our inherent connections with others, we must most fully know and understand how we can utilize our joys, passions, and talents as gifts for ourselves and for the world. Often, our callings can become apparent to us when we quiet ourselves for contemplation, paying attention to where these joys, passions, and natural talents lie, exercising what Charles Handy (1998) has termed "proper selfishness . . . to accept a responsibility for making the most of oneself by, ultimately, finding a purpose beyond and bigger than oneself" (pp. xviii–xix).

The oftentimes nonlinear path to discovering callings has been wonderfully captured in a wise and delightful book by Gregg Levoy (1998). Through the use of personal insights, mythology, and the teachings and learnings of others, Levoy reminds us that once we are able to listen to our souls' whisperings and actively attend to what is going on inside of ourselves, we are better able to attend to the outside as well. He shares about a time in his life when he felt directionless and despondent. One evening, driving home from work, Levoy was listening to the radio and caught the last line of a song, which referred to the "queen of hearts." Getting out of his car, he looked down and saw a playing card—the queen of hearts. Later that same day, in a conversation with a friend, Levoy recounts this strange event. His friend's most assured response resonates with the experiences of many of us: "When you're on the right path, the universe winks and nods at you from time to time, to let you know . . . [and] once you understand that you're on a path at all, you begin to see [signs] everywhere" (p. 109).

Our retreat dialogues and interviews revealed that, for some of us, that "wink and nod" came in the form of a book in a store that seemed to jump off the shelf into our arms, containing the perfect information about a question or an issue with which we had been struggling; for others, every few days or even every day there were confirmations, feedback, that a recently made decision was the right one.

Depending on your interpretation, events like these in your life may be just coincidences. Yet, when they mean something to you, are instructive and guiding, they are best known as *synchronicities.* Synchronicities, a term coined by Carl Jung (1963a), are interconnected happenings that carry messages, much as many now believe our dreams do. Whether they come in the form of coincidences or much more, it is only through being present, paying attention to the people and events in our lives, that we are awake to be aware of our callings.

FINDING MY MISSION THROUGH SELF-KNOWLEDGE

I graduated from college in 1968, which many have called "the year the world stood still." The Tet Offensive in Vietnam, the assassinations of Bobby Kennedy and Martin Luther King Jr., the invasion of Czechoslovakia, the student protests at every major university, the chaos of the Democratic National Convention in Chicago . . . all of this and much more set the stage for political turmoil. With each event, my consciousness of my self and the world grew and grew.

I also started my career at that time. First, I taught in a high school, and then I held a series of positions in nonprofit organizations, almost always working with and for the poor and disenfranchised. I worked in direct service for eight years before my first entry into management. It was a fairly direct, although long, route to the top. I had titles like Program Coordinator, Branch Director, Associate Executive Director, Assistant Vice President, and finally Executive Director and General Secretary.

Indeed, this was a period of enormous personal awakening for me. Not only did the world events cause me to feel extremely disillusioned with the government, but I also discovered the feminist movement . . . and what a discovery that was! It proved for me the truth in the verse from an old song by the Eagles, "Oftentimes, it just turns out that we live our lives in chains, and we never even know we have the keys."

In the 1980s, I experienced a spiritual awakening. Up until then, I was a devout, though disillusioned, Catholic. When I finally realized how deeply the gender divisions in the Church hierarchy ran, severely blockading the possibility of women becoming priests, I walked away. I drifted, but I was searching, especially as a mother with my own young child. I felt the need for a higher guidance—a truthful spiritually—which led me to the Religious Society of Friends (Quakers). In Friends, I found the spiritual home for which I was searching.

Earlier in this book, we talked about wholeheartedness and the authenticity of leadership, and we reinforce these concepts here because they are central to the fulfillment of our missions and our sustainability as leaders. Through authentic leadership, we merge our public and private worlds into a cohesive way of being, which helps us bring forward who we are. McCleod's (2002) description of leadership in Native American communities illustrates this complete integration: "Tribal leadership is the embodiment of a lifestyle, an expression of learned patterns of thought and behaviors, values, and beliefs. Culture is the basis; it formulates the purpose, process, and ultimately, the product" (p. 14). When we are authentic, bringing our whole selves to our leadership, we embody not only who we are now but also all that has come before. We are connected in a profound manner to our inner dreams, goals, and desires, and we can unleash our full power and energy for positive change. It is only then that we are able to advance our missions

> *Knowing that I have been the driving or unifying force that brought perhaps a motley crew of folks together and unified them to see the vision, and see the mission, and help them achieve it; that is truly . . . that's better than anything else . . . to look back and say, 'Wow! We did that!'*
>
> (Interviewee)

What sustains me? Believing in what I do. I grew up in the Deep South, and that made me want to make a difference in the world. My dad died when I was a little kid. That made me want to change the world. It made me want to make sure that everyone in the world has the same chance. That led to where I am. And what sustains me is thinking that what we're doing makes a difference in the lives of people. I can't tell you the number of times that people have called me and said, 'For the first time in years, my mom has hope', 'My dad has hope', 'Can you help my son?' 'Can you help my daughter?' 'Can you help my dad?' 'Can you help my grandmother?' 'Can you help me?' And that makes a difference. It really does.

(Interviewee)

If you don't have the vision and a path to achieve it, you may never get there.

(Interviewee)

and those of our organizations and communities to fulfill both, contributing most meaningfully to the world.

Indeed, living our missions is truly a profound sustaining force. Simply fulfilling our professional aspirations keeps us, as women leaders, going in our jobs. It is important for us to know that what we are doing will contribute something to our world that will last long after we have stepped out of our formal roles, to know that we have played an integral role in the creation of something new and substantive by investing our time and talents.

Although we realize that we can always learn and improve, we need to show up in our jobs, knowing that we are proficient and competent. Understanding and then building upon our strengths, we will continue to develop and grow as individuals and as leaders. This is living and leading authentically. It is leading from a solid foundation, which encourages others to live and lead fully, as well. In so doing, we draw upon our spirits in our work.

The Paradox of Living Our Missions

Yes, for many of us, our mission is the sum of our hopes and ambitions—a calling, a physical or psychological pull to do something or live a certain way. This intuitive or innate drive is seen as living our purpose. Richard Leider (2004) describes this happening when "the recognition of the presence of the sacred within us and the choice of work is consistent with that presence" (p. 11). Some people go through exercises—much like organizations do—to define what they believe their mission is and how they plan to achieve it, using practical and logical means to articulate for themselves and others what they are about and how they plan to engage.

Regardless of how individual leaders come to it and define it, understanding our missions gives us an overarching framework and a gut-level sense to guide us in pursuit of our personal and professional goals. Yet, living them every day brings us face to face with the need to manage their inherent paradoxes, the ability to hold seemingly conflicting realities in our minds and lives.

In his examination of the role that the management of paradoxes plays in a sustainable world, Handy (1994) introduces the paradox of "twin citizenship and subsidiarity" (p. 113). Both are relevant for us as we lead and live our missions. Twin citizenship is the "sense of belonging to something bigger as well as to something smaller" (p. 117). Believing in twin citizenship allows us to accept restrictions on individual independence when it advances the greater good. It helps us balance individual, organizational, and global purposes. Subsidiarity is commonly defined as the principle by which matters are handled by the most local competent authority. It is teamwork; it requires that, as individuals, we take responsibility for ourselves at the same time we develop "mutual confidence" with each other (p. 142). Cultivating mutual confidence depends upon basic human qualities like authenticity, integrity, and character. These qualities support wholehearted leadership and the fulfillment of missions, large and small, system-specific and individual.

Synchronization of mission and action feed sustainability and help this wholeheartedness grow. Harmony with our personal mission promotes personal integrity. At the same time, embodying personal integrity requires courage—courage of conviction, expression, and self. It requires that we be persistent and active in understanding ourselves and the world around us. If we consider the call to leadership as one way of authentically understanding our personal missions, most of us accept that we have a commensurate responsibility to foster balance and sustainability within our organizations and our communities. Yet, what happens when our personal and organizational missions are confusing or incongruent?

Most of us do not knowingly choose to be leaders in arenas where the mission of the system for which we are responsible is antithetical to our personal, stated purposes. However, it is indeed rare that our personal missions and our organizational missions are exactly identical. We can define and live our personal missions, and they may or may not speak directly to our work. In fact, when our missions become our work, we may risk losing our connection to the larger world and threaten our sustainability as well as that of our organizations. When our personal and organizational missions are too closely aligned, the resulting enmeshment can cause us to be ineffectual. We learn and grow from tension and diversity. Without a challenge to push our missions or to view them from a different perspective, they can stagnate and the value of our leadership is diminished accordingly.

> *I struggle constantly feeling that I'm not working hard enough or feeling that I'm not caught up on life, or feeling that I'm not getting time to spend with friends and family. I don't know how you resolve that issue. I guess balance is the largest issue I face. I love what I do—I'm excited about what I do—that makes it easier on the other hand . . . but that doesn't keep me warm at night.*
>
> **(Interviewee)**

We can usually see something about ourselves in the organization's mission. That being said, quite frequently when we do not see resonance between our personal mission and the mission of the organization, we encounter burnout. In truth, burnout is not really from overwork, but rather it is the misalignment between the personal and organizational missions (Porter-O'Grady & Malloch, 2007). And, as we learned from

What I realize now is that we were putting value stakes in the ground; we didn't define it in that way; we were going to run a "good" business . . . We were establishing values. Not by saying what out there might we want to have—we weren't buying things off the shelf. We were looking inside and seeking what was important, pulling it out, getting it on the table, finding out what we all felt about it . . . In so doing, we realized that we could not have a compartmentalized life. I also feel that this is something that I see in women. There is a hunger on the part of a lot of people—men and women—today to lead an integrated life rather than compartmentalized. We said that we have one set of values of our lives, and it is that set of values that we will bring to play in all areas of our lives. We are each one, full human being, and we will bring that whole human being to everything that we do, including business. One of the things that we had heard—we were innocent people in the world of business—veterans had said that "it was hard, but it was a business decision, and I had to do it." And we said, "What does that mean?" It felt to us that there was a different set of rules in the playground of business than in the rest of our lives—not our Sunday, go-to-meetin' values, not the values that we'd bring home to our families and relatives; it's different, and we can be something less here in business. We said we're not doing that.

(Interviewee)

one another, we can go one step further; burnout does not even have to be a misalignment between your mission and that of the organization, it can be between your mission and that of the person to whom you report (supervisor, board of directors, trustees). For us, that is the real meaning of burnout; it is not the endless hours we spend at work, but the result of seemingly irreconcilable misalignment between our organization's (or a department's, division's, etc.) values or those of its leadership and our own "reason for being" in the world.

When the alignment gap is too great, we must take radical action and either change the system or leave the system. If you are not in the position to change the organizational mission, it becomes a matter of survival. However, in many of the situations we explored, we found the existence of low-grade dissonance, more akin to discomfort or ambivalence than fundamental opposition. This is when we most need to understand and manage the paradox of twin citizenship and subsidiarity. We must negotiate for ourselves whether the incongruity we perceive is worth the benefit that our roles in leading these systems offer our organizations, communities, and society.

We must safeguard our integrity and authenticity when we are faced with uneasiness or lack of support to determine for ourselves when enough is enough. Despite their serious nature, moral and ethical dilemmas in the misalignment of missions tend to be the more easily identified conflicts; however, the majority of circumstances are less clear. Again, leaving the organization may be the answer for some; for those who elect to take this route, the decision is often a complex and difficult one. Despite what others say, we can only do it when we are ready; only we, ourselves, know deep down if our work is complete enough.

When we face hostility and difficult challenges that seem to compromise our integrity, one response is to consult our confidants. The words of trusted colleagues are important, yet we doubtlessly receive multiple—often conflicting—opinions about the best course to take. It is paramount that we root ourselves in our purpose and trust our inner selves at each decision point. Making a decision to leave obviously impacts the systems we lead and, although there are no guarantees, we can be certain that staying in an organization when all of who we are screams out to us to leave is not good for ourselves or the systems we lead. Leaving may be the best option, even if the organization therefore dies.

> *Be true to yourself in everything in life. But it's hard these days, it's hard having a career, having a family, all these restrictions, all these obligations . . . follow your heart, do what feels right to you . . . Follow your heart about what is your priority at that time in your life . . . Whatever you're feeling, take a look at that, listen to that and listen to and trust yourself . . . Listen to yourself, and that will put you in good stead in whatever you choose to do, leader or not. Be aware; know yourself. Truly know yourself.*
>
> **(Interviewee)**

However, those of us who stay in our organizations after heartfelt reflection and conscious decision making tend to believe that there is still a lot more work to be done, that continued growth and positive change are possible, and that we retain the capacity to add value to the process without doing too much damage to ourselves. And this is fine—for however long that assessment holds true. It is much worse when we so strongly—and sometimes blindly—feel a commitment to advance our organizational missions knowing that we are losing our way in the process. When this happens, we are no longer taking responsibility for ourselves and, as such, cannot be authentic participants in creating workplaces of mutual trust and confidence. In effect, we are acting in leadership positions, but we are no longer leading—this is ultimately a lose-lose situation.

Internal and External Constellations

As leaders, we must reconcile our internal and external constellations; that is, we must manage the sometimes inherent tension between our personal journeys and those of the organizations or communities that we lead (Collay et al., 2002). Even though we doggedly promote solidarity in the advancement of organizational and community missions, few of us acknowledge that we have a corresponding responsibility to stay centered and do whatever it takes to support and prepare ourselves to make the hard decisions that have to be made by leaders. We often disregard this premise so that we continue to play by organizational rules, even when they no longer seem fair or may even cause harm. When we place precedence on organizational missions that require us to subjugate our personal ones, we do not focus on what would help us, as individuals, best thrive and remain whole. We bury our needs and goals at the expense of our health or happy home life with similar deleterious consequences for our organizations.

In their work with women in academic leadership, Phillips and van Ummersen (2003) found that one reason women seek senior positions in higher education is because they believe that the institutions they lead can be enhanced through an infusion of their personal values, which often center on the importance of achieving balance between their personal and family lives and their careers. When they face challenges, they are sustained by a sense of community, beautifully illustrated through the analogy of the sequoia tree: Despite the grand height of the trees, their root system is surprisingly shallow yet entwined with the roots of the surrounding sequoias (Phillips and van Ummersen, 2003). Held fast by the other trees, growth and endurance are not only possible but outstanding. Simply being part of the forest or the same organization is not enough to sustain us. It is only through the organic process of developing meaningful connections that we build each other up and make ourselves stronger.

Light and Shadow

Personal and organizational missions are unique and interrelated, like the diamonds in our web. They are linked to and reflected in each other. We can survive if they are incongruent only when we are strong and grounded in ourselves and are able to engage the informal and formal supports of our colleagues and teams toward positive values and action. When we are unable to do this, forces for resistance within and outside our systems can overwhelm our missions and visions, again inevitably rendering us less effective in our roles as leaders.

The life of a leader reflects on the system itself. Leaders are role models and represent the face of their organization to the outside world at all times; as one of the retreat participants is fond of saying, "Wherever the leader goes, so goes her organization." In his discussion of the relationship between leadership and spirituality, Palmer (1996) defines a leader this way:

> A leader is a person who has an unusual degree of power to project on other people his or her shadow, or his or her light. A leader is a person who has an unusual degree of power to create the conditions under which other people must live and move and have their being . . . A leader is a person who must take special responsibility for what's going on inside him- or herself, inside his or her consciousness, lest the act of leadership create more harm than good. (p. 35)

With the power that we hold as leaders, we have responsibility to do good. Intentionally or not, leaders set examples and influence people in their organizations and communities. Our values pervade our organizations and, to a degree, conjoin with the broader missions to influence the climate and actions of the systems and their members.

Palmer (1996) agrees, and in asking leaders to address their shadows, a concept explored extensively by Carl Jung (1963b), directly and deeply, he enumerates five of the biggest shadows: insecurity; competition in response to a culture of perceived hostility; overdeveloped responsibility and the belief that we can fix or control everything—if we just try hard enough; denial of death, or the refusal to acknowledge the death of ideas and things that are no longer working; and fear, especially the fear that we will be viewed as failing.

When we let our shadow sides prevail, we abandon ourselves to the divergent energies of the organization. At that point, we are not able to harness the abundance of positive transformational energy that exists within our systems and ourselves. When we are unable to dissipate or transform trapped toxic energy, it manifests itself through illness and the breakdown in relationships, hurting the very systems we are committed to support.

Yet when we care for ourselves, we promote the value of self-care in our systems. When we are wholehearted, we have greater capacity to recognize the importance of others. And when we honestly face our shadow side, as we described earlier in our review of organizational toxicity, we are better able to shed the light on our organizations that they need for growth rather than to suffocate them in darkness.

> *Sometimes when we are authentic, we discover there are parts of us that are really unclean. In terms of trying to achieve a real sense of balance, we have to embrace those parts of ourselves that are our gifts. We have to go in there and embrace the shadow side and recognize that some of the light can come from the shadow side, but if you hold on to it too tightly, it can come back to hurt you.*
>
> **(Retreat participant)**

Faith as the Spirituality of Living Our Missions

When we make decisions from our deepest spiritual place, they fit with our personal missions and help us reconcile our inner and outer constellations. We exhibit our resilience, even in adverse situations. Resilience allows us to get back up after we have been knocked down. It brings an extra dimension of strength to our leadership, and it reconnects us with our spirituality. Chesley (2005) explores the concept of resilience in overcoming injustice, noting that resilient people are highly motivated out of feelings of goodwill, and resilient leaders often are associated with moral action. Their resilience helps them ensure that there is capac-ity to initiate the action necessary to support their missions, sustain and weather unforeseen obstacles, and handle external issues with an appropriate semblance of control. When we embrace our missions, we open ourselves up to embrace the missions of others, and the power of the interconnected pursuit allows us to recreate our organizations and our planet in ways that help us all to thrive.

Rolheiser (1999) describes seven principles of global spirituality that are common among mature spiritual practices across cultures. These practices are grounded in deep nonviolence, solidarity with all life and Earth, and the capacity to live morally. They are implemented through spiritual practice and the mature self-knowledge that yield simplicity of life, selfless service, and prophetic action. These principles reinforce the na-

> *The more connected [we] are in conversation, thinking, and sharing, the more life happens . . . people meditate to go deeper, and organizations need internal conversations to understand who they are and what their missions are, too. This is necessary for growth, and it is a paradox in itself.*
>
> **(Retreat participant)**

ture of sustainable leadership. When we know who we are and how we connect with each other, our work, and the planet, we are best prepared to passionately and positively act and drive change in a way that generates benefits beyond the work itself.

Handy's (1994) discussion of faith and purpose succinctly summarizes this point. He explains that faith has no reasons because if reasons existed, we would not need faith. From this perspective, it is critical for us to believe in our purpose on Earth to live meaningful, fruitful lives just as the centuries-ago laborers who designed and built the earliest cathedrals did. Without knowing whether they would live to see them completed, they worked diligently to contribute to something grand that they could only envision, something that would be a positive force into the future. This approach, while challenging in the here and now, is possible if we build upon the senses of continuity, connection, and direction. Faith becomes possible if and when we believe that the purpose of this life is to live so that others can live better after we are gone, knowing that we will live on in the continuing

> *By walking and living my purpose, the things that are supposed to happen, happen.*
>
> **(Interviewee)**

lives of others. Leading from faith taps into women's ways of knowing there is more, more than immediate and material success, more enduring benefit, and it is essential to our sustainability. As offered by the journalist and public radio host Krista Tippett (2007), "Faith is as much about questioning as it is about certainties" (p. 3).

Cross-Trainings for the Soul

READINGS

▓ Barry Oshry talks about leadership and management from a unique perspective: the middle. His book, *Leading Systems: Lessons from the Power Lab* (1999), is particularly helpful.

▓ Peter Block has several books on leadership that challenge our perception of what can and cannot happen in the workplace, including *Stewardship: Choosing Service over Self-Interest* (1993). Another work, entitled *The Answer to How Is Yes* (2003), helps change the way we frame our problems.

▓ There are many myths and stories that can be found in magazines and on the Web. One intriguing journal is entitled *Parabola: Myth, Tradition and the Search for Meaning*. Published four times a year, each edition is dedicated to one topic. The articles and stories are cross-cultural and relate to the topic chosen for the edition. The Web site for more information is: http://wwww.parabola.org.

REFLECTIONS

▓ Contemplate your purpose. What is your reason for being? Create a personal or leadership mission. Use it as a daily guidepost. What values underlie your mission? What are the core beliefs that are essential to your success in living your mission? What do they look like? How will you know when you are living them? What resources do you have that can help you live your mission and values? What additional resources would be helpful? How can you access them?

▓ Reflect on your shadow side. What challenges your full and authentic leadership? This question can be scary and difficult to consider deeply as it uncovers parts of us we often prefer to deny, at least subtly. One way to get started in this work is to reflect on the five shadows Palmer (1996) defined and we mention in this chapter: insecurity, competition, overdeveloped responsibility and control, denial of death in all aspects of life, and fear. Accept that your shadow side is there. We all have one. It is a natural part of our lives, not wrong or bad, just a part of us. However, as you learn more about your shadow side, expand the reflection to understanding the light you have within you to balance your shadows. Discover ways to enhance your light.

RHYTHMS & RITUALS

▓ *Mandala* is a Sanskrit word loosely translated to mean circle. Circles are used widely in various faith-based and secular traditions to demonstrate wholeness and connection. They are powerful symbols of unity. *Meditating with Mandalas: 52 New Mandalas to Help You Grow in Peace and Awareness* (2005) by David Fontana is a beautiful book that introduces a person to both meditation and the art and history of the mandala. You can also create a personal mandala to deepen into various aspects of your life and discover the circles within (all is connected). Some resources to do this include the Mandala Project at www.mandalaproject.org, mandala coloring books that can be found at many book stores and on the Internet, and sand mandala kits that contain all the ingredients necessary to have a mandala creating evening with seven of your friends or colleagues.

■ Develop insight into your work style by taking the Myers-Briggs Type Indicator, a well-validated and reliable instrument. This can also be done by our staff colleagues to determine how people best process information, helping everyone to better understand themselves and one another as they do their work. There are a number of Web sites, but here are two possibilities: http://www.discoveryourpersonality.com, and http://www.personalitypathways.com. You can take this yourself online, however the greater benefit is to do it as a workgroup with a trained facilitator. Another personality inventory that gives insight into both performance and work style is the Enneagram. A Web site to explore is www.enneagraminstitute.com. This process will also give you insight into yourself, and how you relate to others and they to you.

CHAPTER SEVEN

Personal and Organizational Balance and Boundaries

Women in leadership roles can help restore balance and wholeness to our communities.

—Wilma Mankiller

During our retreats, one of the most powerful metaphors that we discussed was the Mobius strip (Palmer, 2004).[1] Parker Palmer refers to the Mobius strip as a "Quaker PowerPoint" (p. 10) because it can be demonstrated by taking a strip of paper, forming it into a circle, and then twisting it so that it looks like a figure eight or the infinity sign (see Figure 3). When you do this, you realize that the outside is inside and the inside is outside. Mobius Products and Services, a company that makes this figure into a necklace, cleverly has as their company motto: "There's only one side and we're all on it."

The mathematical symbol of the Mobius strip connects us back to our Earthview principle that all is one; it is a metaphoric reality that illustrates the interconnected way of life. The Mobius strip clearly contrasts with Western culture in which everything is separate, different,

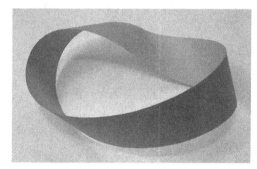

FIGURE 3 Mobius Strip

and stratified into layers. In the workplace, our roles and responsibilities may seem very different, but when we think about the Mobius strip, we realize that we fit together in circular or spiral, rather than hierarchical, relationships.

---

[1]The Mobius strip was discovered in 1858 by German mathematician and astronomer August Ferdinand Mobius. The mathematical equation that produces the shape is known as a Mobius transformation or bilinear transformation. The Mobius strip is a fascinating sacred geometric shape. Its one-sided surface flows from inner to outer and back again, expressing the continuous journey along with the pathway of life. It is a symbol of no duality. It appears to have two sides yet has only one.

By truly internalizing and appreciating the connections throughout our environment—between and among others, as well as within and "with-out" ourselves—we gain insight into the complexities of our lives. When these relationships become coherent, we can discover and tell our own truths, rejoining soul and role (Palmer, 2004). Our outlook shifts, and we become more thoughtful of our actions and behaviors as we appreciate how they impact our relationships with others. And, consequently, our workplaces change. We redirect that energy, and the atmosphere of the work environment is something we all create. A welcoming environment originates in our willingness to be open and responsive to others so that we can see ourselves in them and them in us.

To help others build these relationships, we must build them for ourselves. But how do we do this and not endanger our sustainability as leaders? Making time for this type of leadership requires taking time for ourselves. It is difficult to be grounded and self-sufficient, especially when we seem to be continually thrown off balance.

As leaders, we need to establish and maintain strong yet permeable boundaries between ourselves and the organizations we lead. It is easy for us to invest our personal selves in an organization at unhealthy levels so that we are, as one woman leader said, negotiating a piece of ourselves rather than working through an issue. We need to clarify our distinct roles within our organizations at the same time that we become one with them. We need to connect with them and help connect them with the world, even while we are simultaneously being set apart and even isolated as leaders. Additionally, we must constantly strive to reclaim a sense of centeredness that aligns our personal and professional lives in the face of seemingly divergent and competing demands from outside and within organizational structures that are often rigid in their power dynamics and political complexities.

So, what does it mean to establish boundaries? As healthy individuals, our core responsibility is to live our lives; we cannot live for two people. Yet often, as leaders, our boundaries become so flimsy that we start to resemble a slice of Swiss cheese, with lots of holes made by our constant giving and others taking. It is true that

> *It's kind of like rock climbing—as long as there are three things to hang on to (home, understanding peers, faith)—you can cope with one going off, but not two.*
>
> **(Interviewee)**

> *Some of the lessons I would want to pass on—to be transparent, to communicate, and to use humor. Humor about oneself is a great resource; it breaks down the ice. Whatever the personality. And to over-communicate. To stay focused on the purpose. When all of the blaming comes, to stay focused on purpose, and to let everything pass by. Anticipate resistance. We plan for it. We gather forces to deal with it. We are willing to change what we're trying to accomplish to bring in resistance and make that part of our solution. It's all how we deal with people and if we are genuinely willing to incorporate [their ideas] when possible. To be up-front if it's not possible. Those are major lessons for any experience.*
>
> **(Interviewee)**

our boundaries need to be permeable, but they have to exist. Healthy boundaries (as learned from family therapists and organizational system thinkers and reaffirmed by the Earthview) simultaneously hold us together and keep us apart. This paradox becomes more important when we think about the difference between caring for and taking care of someone. As women leaders, we are inclined to do the latter. When we find ourselves with more holes than substance, again, like the cheese, we become hard, rigid, and more easily broken. When we become more aware, we realize that what really needs our caring is our own spirit. When you are spirit-less, you cannot care for yourself or anyone else. Healthy, appropriately porous, flexible boundaries are indeed necessary to remain whole—self-caring, balanced, and centered.

In stressful or predatory environments, we must manage the internal tension between compassion and the struggle to achieve balance, all the while being conscious to shield ourselves from danger. Boundaries, like a cover of soil, can help achieve this balance and protect our roots. Without appropriate balance and boundaries, we are unprotected from whatever harshness and contamination exist in the systems we are trying to lead. We leave ourselves open to absorbing the effects of unrealistic expectations and our attempts to ease others' pain. Our boundaries need to be firm enough to offer protection as they help clarify who we are as women and as leaders. At the same time, they must be permeable enough to let nutrients flow through them and allow for growth, rather than becoming inflexible and unyielding barriers to effective leadership, encouraging isolation and shutting us off from the very systems we are trying to lead. Without nutrients from the outside, whatever is inside ultimately dies.

> *Getting balance is so important and so hard for me. I feel a sense of urgency around this work. I have to figure out how to pace myself! It's so hard for me to do one thing at a time.*
>
> (Interviewee)

COMING HOME TO NATURE

Our time together challenged us to feed our souls so that we could survive and thrive as leaders. We know that nature survives and thrives through cycles—cycles of light and darkness, of heat and cold, of birth and death. Sometimes, we have to let go of things. To remain healthy, some things have to die before they can be reborn.

During one of our facilitated *Sustaining Our Spirits* experiences, we were invited to think deeply about what in each of us needs to be nurtured—what needs to be pruned. We were asked, "What are the things that are dying that you are trying to make survive?" "What are the tiniest sprouts that need light to come forward?" "What are you keeping in the dark with all your clutter?" We received the charge to take several hours by ourselves to walk and just *be* in the woods, a place of beauty and safety where pruning, dying, sprouting, and rebirth happen all of the time.

Typically, in our world of work, we hold an unreasonable expectation of growth—of our economy, our companies, our programs—so that thriving simply means doing more, more, and more. From the woods, we learn that this is not so. Being with nature in our retreats, we remembered.

People will challenge and work to convince woman of the value of the distractions and try and make you feel guilty if you fail in your quota of 'woman stuff.' Men are expected to work. You cannot be a good leader if you do not set a high standard. You have to decide where you draw the boundaries. You have to decide that work is critical and you must be serious about your work time. This should become a mantra when you work at home and/or telecommute as part of your work schedule.

(Interviewee)

Centered, sustainable leadership might be about saying yes to some new initiatives, but it also may be about saying yes to cutting back or saying no to doing too many things. It is about centered discernment or an ability to clearly see one's self and one's place in the universe while at the same time recognizing that everything is connected and constantly in flux.

We gleaned many lessons for appreciating our strengths and weaknesses, our most powerful and vulnerable selves, from nature. We realized that we needed to turn our glance inward to discover what is rotting, what is growing wild, what needs to be pruned, and what needs sustenance to flourish. What we sought and discovered was a centeredness—our spirituality—which we can tend through an intricate web of boundaries and balance. We aspired to a deeply rooted balance that was healthy, grounded, and on which other things would grow. It might ebb and flow like the tides or bend this way or that with the wind, but it always would be part of our inner world, just as the oceans and the trees are always here for us.

Because of the interconnected nature of our world, we cannot relegate our spirituality solely to our very deep core beings. Our inner world naturally impacts and influences our interactions with others. The various levels that we need to address as we lead have been described at the United Nations in terms of a triple bottom line, which provides balance for people, organizations, and the Earth. These three aspects include:

1. Ecology or eco-logos (environment): Understanding the household, from the microcosm of my own person to that of the entire planet.
2. Economics or eco-nomos: Managing the household, from personal to global decisions.
3. Equity or equus: Understanding the social implications of our decision making from the personal to planetary.

The metaphor that has been used by several sources, including the United Nations Environment Programme, the United Nations Commission on Sustainable Development, as well as Thomas Berry, Brian Swimme, Mary Evelyn Tucker, and John Grimee, for these three aspects of sustainable development for Earth and humans is that of the three-legged stool. When all three legs are in place, the stool is in balance and will safely hold a person or an object. If decisions are made without consideration of these three aspects, someone or something will not be in balance, consequently throwing off the entire structure and system. When we consider our leadership through the lens of our spirituality, we are better able to achieve this balance and understand our connections with others and the world.

When our thoughts, actions, and being truly originate from our center, we are able then to be present in every moment. This does not mean that we have to be in the presence—all the time—of our family members, friends, and colleagues. Paradoxically, however, it does mean that when we are with others, we need to be present to them, but we may not (and do not have to) always be available at every moment to be in their presence. The practice of mindfulness develops in us the ability to be present at every moment to those who are present.

Moving forward, we realized that we needed to create fresh ways of seeing, understanding, and being in our organization that allowed for both the connectedness of life as well as our need for balance. Our sojourn together and with other women has begun to lay out a path to a new paradigm for organizations and leaders. Courageous spirituality challenges us to set an innovative direction as leaders and brings this path to light in a world where organizations seem to have gone mad.

To do this, it is helpful, once again, to frame our organizations within the Earthview. Consider the weather. Sometimes pleasant, sometimes unpleasant, it is unpredictable and can wreak havoc on our seemingly stable lives. Despite our desire for comfort and familiarity, our organizational systems behave in a similar way. Turbulence and complexity are inherent in organizational environments, which are impacted in great and small ways by behaviors within and outside them. Wheatley (2005, 2006) reframes much of what has been traditionally espoused in leadership literature by directing leaders to connect with organizational turbulence rather than fight it. For example, she writes:

> As times grow more chaotic, as people question the meaning (and meaninglessness) of this life, people are clamoring for their leaders to save and rescue them . . . People press their leaders to do anything to end the uncertainty, to make things better, to create stability . . . No leader can achieve this and it drains energy out of those who try. (2005, p. 126)

As leaders, one of our goals is to focus on finding ways to positively connect people with the chaos and turbulence they perceive and to help them become balanced within the unpredictability of our systems and our lives. Just as the Earth and all that of which it is comprised are interdependent, so, too, are our organizations. Finding ways to reconnect them with the realities of themselves breathes life into them, inspires, and helps them

I think that a leader is someone who has a basic set of values that they live and that radiates from them. Integrity is one of my big ones—what do you do when no one is watching? Honesty goes along with integrity. Being fair to everyone, embracing diversity . . . understanding that the mission is the thing that brings us all together, even though we might not always agree with it, it's the one unifying force that allows us to internalize and then communicate to everyone else what the details of the mission are and to reinforce and move towards the goal. A leader is all of those things.

(Interviewee)

> *Read something every day . . . You have to do something that feeds your mind every day. You have to read something, and read something that you ordinarily wouldn't . . . For me, I pick up the engineering magazines; I have no idea of what they're thinking. And just yesterday, I found out that engineers use the word 'agile' totally differently than you or I would. They have a totally different frame of reference for that one word. So, for me, that is fascinating.*
>
> **(Interviewee)**

> *Do it for yourself and for every woman leader who comes after you! Our culture will beat you into the ground if you let it. SO DON'T! Take care of yourself. You need thinking time, fun time, learning time, and contemplative time.*
>
> **(Retreat participant)**

thrive. Rather than sealing off dysfunctional parts, which actually heightens problems, we need to reinforce the ties that unite them with the whole. This attention energizes and offers the resources needed to promote more healthful growth and development.

Radical Self-Care

To negotiate the tensions of boundaries, giving, and balance in our interconnected world, we understand that courage is necessary and that our work will never be complete. Yet, we can begin. To offer guidance and support for others, we have to seek and live out our lives with *radical self-care*, a term used in many arenas—from anthropology to massage therapy—to describe activities that center us and bring us balance.

During a conversation with a group of Quaker women leaders, one of us queried, "What would you do if you knew that the part of you that craved joy was God speaking to you?" The answers culminated with the recognition that for women it is, indeed, radical to accept that notion and to truly take the time to enhance the experience of joy and self-nurturing. As they discussed what sustained them, they generated a list of activities that seemed almost more like chores than life-giving opportunities: going to the gym, reading, and hiking in the woods. The conversational energy shifted dramatically when the women were asked, "What would you do if you were to get really radical in caring for yourself?" They would laugh a lot, dance to rock and roll, sew, get great sleep, walk around naked, play in a band, create a beautiful space for self, have more sex (or other orgasmic activities), eat chocolate, and have leather furniture. What would you do?

Radical self-care helps us find the personal resilience to be calm and centered in the face of almost anything. Activities and rituals that feed our souls give us space and time to integrate our light and shadow sides. They help us understand, fundamentally, that we have purpose, and they help us regain our purpose when and if it gets lost. As leaders, it is our responsibility to continuously engage in our own radical self-care to stay connected with our purpose. Doing so helps us to be better able to step into our own elemental waters and return to our place of authentic power, allowing us to most fully be able to maintain our voice and hear those of others.

YOU HAVE TO BE THE ONE TO TAKE CARE OF YOU!

All of the participants in the *Sustaining Our Spirits* initiative were at different places in their careers. Some were in new positions; some had accumulated several years of leadership in positions that were extraordinarily difficult; and some had reached the end of their tenure—ready to move on.

I discovered really quickly that participating with this group was one of the most important things I had ever done. While it seems cliché to say that it saved my professional life, I know that it did. By connecting my life's journey to that of others, I was able to gain insight from our similar and shared experiences. I also learned that it was really important to set aside a block of time to do this with intentional spiritual grounded-ness.

The most important thing I learned is that I have to be the one to take care of me! No one else can or will do it for me. Our culture can beat us into the ground—if we let it, so I learned not to! I learned that to take care of myself, I need time—time to think, time for fun, time to learn, time to contemplate, time for radical self-care. So now, I ensure that my busy schedule does not rob me of my right to time and this care.

Cross-Trainings for the Soul

READINGS

■ All of the works by Peter Senge and his associates are incredibly valuable resources, including *The Fifth Discipline: The Art and Practice of the Learning Organization* (1990); *The Fifth Discipline Fieldbook: Strategies and Tools for Building a Learning Organization* (Senge, Kleiner, Roberts, Ross, & Smith, 1994); *The Dance of Change: The Challenges to Sustaining Momentum in Learning Organizations* (Senge, Kleiner, Roberts, Roth, et al., 1999); and *Presence: Human Purpose and the Field of the Future* (Senge, Scharmer, Jaworski, & Flowers, 2004). Senge's work is open-ended and continues to break new ground in addressing the difficulties of leadership in a global society. See the Web site of the Society for Organizational Learning, http://www.solonline.org, for an overview of his work and excerpts from his books and those of his colleagues.

■ Work by Senge's colleague, C. Otto Scharmer, can be found at http://www. ottoscharmer.com. He has just published a book on Theory U (2007). These theories of organizational change are helpful to give perspective on the ups and downs that are found in all businesses and organizations—not for profit and for profit.

■ Parker Palmer is a Quaker and mystic. His writings, such as *A Hidden Wholeness: The Journey Toward an Undivided Life* (2004), are informative as well as comforting. The wisdom found in his books is a treasure for the soul.

REFLECTIONS

■ Think about a time when you felt particularly balanced, centered. Try to remember all the details of this experience. Where were you? What were you doing? Who was with you? Sit quietly as you remember and try to reconnect with that feeling. Stay with it for as long as you can. What can you learn from that experience that you can bring forward with you? What are the core principles and practices that you can build more into your life?

■ Deeply consider the United Nations' triple bottom line: ecology, economics, and equity. How do they apply to your life and work? What valence/importance do you give to each of these? Why? Why not?

RHYTHMS & RITUALS

■ Physical exercise is a great way to incorporate ritual into daily life and to derive proven physical, emotional, and spiritual benefits. Discover the power of physical exercise to restore your body and your soul, to support the connection of mind, body, and spirit. Experiment with different ways of moving and find at least one that works well for you. *The Chemistry of Joy: A Three-Step Program for Overcoming Depression Through Western Science and Eastern Wisdom* (Emmons, 2006) explores the link between exercise and emotional well-being and offers an exciting resource for understanding what types of exercise might be best for you based on your body chemistry. Opportunities might include mindful walking, swimming, tai chi, yoga, or another modality that centers and uplifts you.

■ Engage in guided imagery, a gentle and effective practice that allows you to focus on your senses and center your imagination, forging a mind-body-spirit connection that can help heal and heighten your creativity. We find the work of Belleruth Naparstek to be among the very best. Her tapes are soothing and restorative. Visit her at http://www.healthjourneys.com/.

Dis-Covering Community

Call it a clan, call it a network, call it a tribe, call it a family;
whatever you call it, whoever you are, you need one.

—Jean Howard

Early leadership conversations in our retreats often hovered lightly around the question of community and the importance of relationships. Initially, these topics felt a bit uncomfortable for some of us; the misalignment between our espoused valuing of connections and finding ways to enact that while living in a culture that so highly prizes individualism and the strength to be on one's own became glaringly apparent. Nevertheless, as we opened up to one another, we realized that community was indeed foundational to our leadership and our relationships.

During our retreats, we reflected on the word *community*—especially as *com-unity*—which highlights its meaning of being one in unity. We realized that rather than being monolithic, true communities are whole like a garden, a life-giving ecosystem where each aspect—soil, water, sun, and plants—works in harmony with each other to co-create the best garden possible. In particular, one of our rituals was to reflect on *The Japanese Garden* (Aserappa, 1999), a book filled with metaphors and Taoist wisdom, which blended the garden image with that of leadership. After a period of quiet, we came back with our own metaphors that described ourselves and our leadership roles.

This simple exercise brought us to another place of understanding and opportunity to embody and enact the qualities that emerged from our sharing. We came to believe that when we view our unity as many parts making up the whole, our work may not become easier but it will have more meaning, substance, and rewards that are generated from our opportunities to grow in relationships with others. Our work

> *You can have a very bold, creative, and compelling vision, but you can't achieve that vision alone. You have to engage others in that vision, and it's about collaborating and co-creating with them.*
>
> **(Interviewee)**

becomes co-laboring rather than being an individual product by each person separated from the others in cubicles. The resulting meaning and mindfulness then become the essence of the community that we find with one another, subsequently creating networks and webs that reach far beyond the capacity of any single individual.

By authentically sharing with each other throughout the retreats and the writing process, we discovered—as we had hoped—that our connection served as a source of nourishment for us. We began to explore how, as leaders, we could create an ecosystem that supports the mission of our work as well as the well-being of our co-workers. The opportunity to come together, share, discuss, bounce ideas around, and even vent among other women leaders was one of the founding intentions of the group, and it emerged as one of its central benefits, challenges, and joys. Therefore, it is not surprising that the chance to belong to a community that validates and fosters connection within self and among others repeatedly surfaced in our interviews as being one of women leaders' central desires. Unfortunately, however, most workplaces—especially those in the public sphere—do not often offer safe spaces for women to come together, share, and grow.

What sustains me? I'm just beginning to realize this more and more: other women leaders. And many times, we have similar experiences. We want to be seen as a leader—not a female leader, not a woman leader, not a leader who happens to be a woman—we want to be a leader. But we need to be realistic—we are women. There happen to be some things that are different about the way we think; the way we act; the way we're perceived . . . and to be able to get together with other women, and share those experiences, and insights, and help one another out, that's one of the big things that sustains me.

(Interviewee)

Although perhaps not on such a personal level, women's alliances throughout history have offered important avenues for women to work together and achieve goals. From spelling bees and prayer meetings, through the creation of settlement houses and suffrage activist groups, to women's rights movement networks, women's organizations have been critical havens for women, offering the resources necessary for them to develop interest, awareness, and change in their environments. Although it is important to recognize the individuality and diversity of the women within these collectives, communal spirit and action have been especially critical factors in encouraging and achieving change. Some women—feeling alienated from traditional, patriarchal religions—have created alternative spiritual groups, which often focus on connectedness with Earth, ecological awareness and protection, and artistic expression. This sense of community—of belonging to something larger than oneself—counters feelings of loneliness, isolation, and exclusion, which many women feel in male-dominated environments.

Contrary to our usual way of understanding, true communities are discovered, not made. Here, the authentic sharing of stories, experiences and emotions, questions and beliefs lead us to dis-covering the "shared story," the real "tie that binds." For, in the words of Mary Daly (1985), "The deepest possible community [is] the community that is discovered, rather than 'formed,' when we meet others who are on the same voyage" (p. 159).

LOCATION, LOCATION, LOCATION . . . FINDING COMMUNITY

Place has a profound impact on how a group interacts. What happened when our *Sustaining Our Spirits* group changed the setting for our gatherings? For our third retreat, we met in a new location—a city. The interaction of our group was less modulated. Some individuals felt out of sync with the rhythms of the city, while others were comforted by the sights and sounds. We interacted in a more confrontational way—challenging one another to decisions about patterns that were cherished by some but perceived by others to be unhealthy. Earlier, we had talked about "landscape" and "habitat" as important components of our spiritual renewal, and through the change in location, we saw clearly how significantly landscape impacts relationships.

As a group, we seemed to move to another level of participation and interaction with one another. In some instances, relationships that had seemed strong began to show signs of stress. In other situations, the opposite was true—bonds were forged and new paths were chosen. Somewhat unexpectedly, through this paradoxical encounter with place, the importance of boundaries became clear.

As we have discussed, engaging in life through the Earthview perspective also encourages the discovery of community. The view of Earth from outer space affirms the community of our planet, as everything—water, land, air, and fire—is interconnected and interdependent, just as each of our lives intertwine. Whether we are conscious of them or not, our relationships with others already exist and continuously evolve; it is up to us to perceive these connections in our lives. When we do so, we act in greater communion with Earth.

Women leaders often suffer from a prevailing sense of being alone; in our retreats, however, we fully appreciated the reality of our inherent relationship with others. Through exercises designed to bring forth some of our personal connections, we discovered there are innumerable people and spirits who help us move forward every day. It was an exciting and comforting revelation. We recognized that the past becomes the present, and we are all connected to the future. No matter where we are, we do not stand alone. We are here because of the hardships and accomplishments of the women who came before us, our mothers, our grandmothers, our role models. We are here because of the women who sit beside us, our sisters, our female and male colleagues, our friends. We are here because of the women who will come after us, our daughters, their daughters, and their daughters. We come from struggle and achievement, and it fills us with hope for the future. And someday women may be sitting in a circle talking about us!

Networks of Women

When we consider the relationships throughout our lives, we see that we have incredible resources available for us to build a foundational network of women leaders. These networks provide support to maintain morale, positive drive, and enthusiasm and to sustain intellectual passion. One interviewee compared the network of women who support her to female dolphins. When a dolphin is pregnant, the other female dolphins in her community surround her and lift her up to the surface of the water so that she can

It's having a kitchen cabinet . . . People who are in similar lines but are older; mentors who have different skills . . . I wish someone would have told me that earlier . . . I do this for others. It doesn't mean that we meet regularly, but it means that we call each other when we need them. I had a kitchen cabinet person with whom I walked around the lake every Friday morning. I spent the whole three miles just letting it rip. Letting this person think with me about options. I felt like a million bucks after I got into my car; I knew I had options. So that's very important to be part of a kitchen cabinet.

(Interviewee)

keep her airhole open and breathe as she gives birth. She never asks for the help, but the other females automatically rally around her.

Similarly, many indigenous cultures value communal relationships and support throughout life, especially during major milestone events. As an example, Native American children are taught to drum and to dance in ritual celebrations with the guidance of an adult member. As the children grow, they are able to drum and dance on their own, yet still as part of the community, knowing that in the future they will serve as a mentor drummer or dancer for future generations.

Networks of women offer a sounding board for thoughts, hopes, frustrations, challenges, and joys. They counter loneliness and are one of the forms of support desired most often by women leaders. Most important, networks open a safe space for women to help others and themselves, to understand and learn from each other, to trust in the abilities of women, and to take care of each other and themselves.

Building Bridges through Storytelling

As we discuss a bit later, even hearing the stories from individuals from our past can offer us guidance and lessons of leadership. In addition to drawing inspiration from these stories, we ensure that great strides are not forgotten when we pass them along. As Diarmuid O'Murchu (2007) has said,

> We are a people with a memory, embodied in myths and narratives that we embrace in our story-telling. But our memory has been deranged and our story has been dismembered. Our deep connections with creation's story have been fragmented and desecrated. (p. 59)

Telling stories gives women agency and autonomy—women can describe their lives and experiences without someone doing it for them. We can look back in history to encounter these stories, paying homage to the individuals who have struggled to pave the way for women in leadership.

Many ancient cultures honored a female deity and were structured around feminine principles, which were egalitarian, democratic, and peaceful. The inherent value attributed to women eventually diminished, however, as earlier cultures morphed into male-dominated political states in which occupational specialization, social stratification, commerce, and militarism prevailed. As men gained control of social and political forces and women's political, social, and religious authorities grew limited, the power and stories of women were correspondingly diminished or destroyed (Chicago,

1979). This change is evident in the morphing foci of myths, legends, and images of the goddess over time: First, the goddess's original primacy gave way to subordination to male gods; then she was altered and all her rituals and temples transferred to male figures. Finally, the Judeo-Christian tradition absorbed all deities into a single male God.

Nevertheless, women did find ways to have influences and serve as leaders. For example, one of the bright lights during the Middle Ages was the system of abbesses. Abbesses had the rights and privileges of feudal barons. They often administered vast lands and managed convents, abbeys, and monasteries; they provided their own troops in wartime, had the right to coinage, and were consulted in religious and civil affairs (Chicago, 1979). Although these opportunities were eliminated during the Reformation, various innovative and strong women were able to emerge as leaders in the following centuries, especially those who had access to education and economic privilege.

Over the past 200 years, opportunities for women to participate equally in society have gradually opened. Mary Wollstonecraft and other thinkers during the Enlightenment period called for women to receive a place of dignity and worth. Susan B. Anthony and Elizabeth Cady Stanton, among others, organized the Convention on the Rights of Women in Seneca Falls, New York, beginning the modern women's movement, and Sojourner Truth spoke out extensively about the liberation of both blacks and of women. Some women, such as Mary Parker Follett, author of *Creative Experience* (1924) and one of the most prescient 20th-century thinkers, even boldly spoke out about leadership and management. These women, joined by many more, planted the seeds for the future development of women's rights; by doing so, they stand as beacons of light from history who inspire us. They have been joined by women from more contemporary times whose stories we must continue to tell.

I simply needed to open a business bank account—no loans—just the account, and I needed to buy checks with my business's name on them. I went to the bank with my mother—she was my bookkeeper and office manager when we started because she had just retired from her job and my father had passed away; she and I and my other business partner, a female, went to the bank to open a bank account. This was 1979. So, the banker looked at us and smiled and said, 'So, you girls are opening a business! That is so nice. Are you married?' . . . 'Oh, no? Well, does your father know that you're doing this?' And my then-65-year-old mother, who had been in the workforce for 30 years—and he didn't know that she was my mother—sat up and leaned forward and said, 'These young women do not need anyone's permission to do this. Let's just get this bank account opened.'

(Interviewee)

Especially since the 1960s, Western culture has increasingly accepted the ability of women to make choices about their lives. Although disparities still exist—a woman makes, on average, only 76 cents for every dollar earned by man in a comparable position—young (and even not-so-young!) women take for granted many of their opportunities to participate in society. This is reflected in the willingness of women to use the word *feminist*. Women who participated in the women's liberation movement often use this word proudly—being a feminist means supporting women's ability to choose their life's course of action. Many women in the generations following the women's liberation movement do not identify with "feminist," however, and some actually spurn it, claiming, as one interviewee said, that it "is an old hippy word from the 60s and 70s . . . that means you hate men . . . a bra-burning, strident, bitchy woman." Although younger generations of women may not experience the same boundaries and challenges that previous generations encountered, it is nevertheless important for them to acknowledge and appreciate the great strides that have been made and that continue to be needed.

Cross-Trainings for the Soul

READINGS

▥ David Ausberger's *Conflict Mediation Across Cultures: Pathways and Patterns* (1992) provides scenarios and examples of cross-cultural conflicts and possible resolutions.

▥ Riane Eisler has given a look backward and forward in helping us reconstruct a time of "partnership" societies in *The Chalice and the Blade: Our History, Our Future* (1990). This book has great information for dealing with challenges for connecting on a planetary level today in a collaborative, partnership way. Her second book, *The Partnership Way: New Tools for Living and Learning* (2nd ed.) (Eisler & Loye, 1998) is a practical handbook with exercises and examples of ways to get beyond dominator/hierarchical thinking to create a new, more equitable world. Visit her Web site, http://www.partnershipway.org.

▥ A book of strategies for women in leadership, *The Princessa: Machiavelli for Women* (1998) by Harriet Rubin, takes some of the traditional male maxims and inverts them. It is interesting and clever and may provide a smile along the way as well.

REFLECTIONS

▥ Reflect on the myth of the Sumerian goddess, Inanna. She serves as an interesting role model for women leaders. Her myth is one of a woman, knowing she was to be queen, who sought power and took it. Her rule was one of fecundity and peace. However, she knew that to be fulfilled, she had to go deeper, and because of this, she was called to make a descent to her dark sister, Ereshkigal. The women in our retreat and writing group, as did many of the interview participants, understood well the price that women in leadership pay. Using the story of Inanna for reflection on your own journey as leader can aid understanding the symbolic and mythic aspect to which all leaders are called.

▥ Combine reflection and ritual through the practice of Zen eating in community. Prepare a meal of fresh, organic, vegetarian food with several friends. Begin with a brief sharing of gratitude for all the people and natural processes that helped bring the food to your table. Focus on the food as part of the chain of life and as part of that which supports us in our life's mission. Eat in silence with deep appreciation for the food, its shapes, color, smell, taste, and texture. This may be a bit uncomfortable, but with each bite savor the food and let the fullness of the flavor fill you. After the meal and cleanup, share time with your friends reflecting on the experience.

RHYTHMS & RITUALS

▥ Travel can be a piece of your inner growth and cultivation of balance. It may even serve as a mini-sabbatical, giving you several weeks to refresh your mind, body, and soul. Consider a mission trip to share your service and resources; embark on a mythic journey; take a cultural tour that has as its focus understanding the culture, beauty, and wisdom of the people to be visited; take off-the-beaten-track adventures to places that offer a deeper understanding of nature, culture, and leadership possibilities— cycle across Italy, follow the migration of polar bears in the Arctic, or spend some time at a monastery. And study a new language and speak to others in their native language. Make our tendency toward mono-lingualism part of our history, not our future.

▥ Explore activities at home that can broaden your understanding and knowledge of the diversity of the community in which you live.

Connecting the Present and the Future through Role Models and Mentoring

What we have is because someone stood up before us. What our Seventh Generation will have will be a consequence of our actions today.

—Winona LaDuke

Who has enriched your spirit? Who sustains your spirit? One of the primary reasons that we came together to reflect upon women in leadership roles was to gather lessons and words of wisdom that we could disseminate to future women leaders to help enrich and sustain their spirits.

It is strikingly clear that none of us grew into our leadership positions alone. Not only did we gain advice from and work and share our joys and challenges with others, but we also looked toward women—both within our immediate time and place and throughout history—for guidance in various areas of our lives. We also realized that in our leadership roles we serve as guiders and advice givers to others.

Sources of Guidance

We recognize that there are a range of people to whom others look for inspiration and counsel: heroes, role models, coaches, and mentors, to name a few. To foster deeper discussion among ourselves around these different types of individuals, we laid out basic definitions of hero, role model, coach, and mentor. Although the

> *I stand on the shoulders of my people. My grandmother was a teacher and a principal in this school system. And she's now 94 years old. She always went back to her spirituality to ground her. You can lead through your values . . . your beliefs. If you don't . . . this work is too darn hard!*
>
> **(Interviewee)**

lines between them somewhat blur, the definitions provide a modest framework for further exploration.

HEROES

For us, heroes are individuals whose actions and qualities inspire us and provide energy for our lives and our work. In direct contrast to the "ruthless hero" (Csikszentmihalyi, 1997), the heroes we spoke about in our retreats lived their lives in a way that allowed them to leave behind something that reminds us of their impact on the world (Michalko, 2006). They shared characteristics with those described by the women interviewed: they know themselves—their talents and areas "under construction"; they have walked a past path paved with threats and even realized dangers to their own well-being; and they have emerged more aware of self and of others and more caring than when they started. Their spoken values are evident in their actions and interactions. These "empowered and empowering" individuals (Campbell, 1949) are both public and private figures—from Mother Teresa to my Mom. Just knowing their life stories enriched our own.

ROLE MODELS

We define role models as individuals whose broader life course we strive to follow. These individuals inspire and give us guidance based on not only their career choices and successes but also their personal life choices. They may be people we know intimately or celebrated women and men from the past or present whose lives we admire from afar. As we engaged with each other around the stories of people who inspire us, we developed a long list of attributes we believe role models possess: knowledge, wisdom, integrity, courage, understanding, audacity, motivation, and encouragement. We all agreed that cultivating these attributes not only helps us to work more effectively, but, more important, it helps us to become better people. The women (and men) who serve as our role models have been generous in sharing their traits, experiences, and approaches with others to help develop their passions and talents. Of course, we do not intend to copy their lives or to emulate them precisely, but our role models lead lives in ways that give us guidance and hope, even if we only selectively consider certain aspects of their lives as touchstones for our inspiration or for holistic spiritual guidance.

AWAKENING

My mom was the single most important influence on my life. She was smart, funny, and full of love. I don't think a day went by that she didn't hug me and tell me she loved me—that's quite a foundation for growing up!

We talked about politics around the supper table, and our home became a second home for many of our neighborhood friends. My summers were spent reading library books, swimming in the local city pool, and going to the playground. In some ways, my childhood can be considered as "ideal." I never realized we didn't have a lot of money.

However, there was a dark cloud, and, because of it, I experienced one of the defining moments in my life. My dad was an alcoholic and he was abusive—not to me or my brother, but to my mother. I remember vividly watching out the window when he would come home late from work; I could tell by the way his feet came out of the car whether or not he was drunk. I remember sitting on the top step listening to the arguments.

Finally, one night when I was about 11 years old, my mom had had enough. My dad was particularly bad that night, and she picked up the phone and called the police—sobbing and asking them to arrest my father.

My dad was taken away and spent the night in jail. And lo and behold, he returned to our home as a changed man. He didn't drink anymore, and our family life became so much stronger. Over the years, when I have told friends who have had an alcoholic parent this story, they wonder how their lives would have been if their parents had the courage to stand up, as mine did. This was a defining moment for who I would become as an adult.

COACHES

Coaches principally provide professional guidance. In this relationship, the interaction is often unidirectional. Generally, coaches are external consultants who can provide an objective perspective from outside of our organizations, often related to a particular issue or skill for development. They are typically paid to provide this service.

MENTORS

Although certain aspects of mentoring might spill over into the personal realm, we see mentors as primarily professional guides. Mentors listen to our ideas and offer objective feedback. They might help us with issues of balance, model social interactions (Casto, Caldwell, & Salazar, 2005), introduce us to networks of individuals in positions of higher authority, or even aim to prepare us for career succession (Murphy, 2004). Their interactions with us may be formal, through an orchestrated mentoring program or a relationship with regular interaction, or informal, through a natural relationship that develops with more sporadic interaction about professional concerns. Unlike coaching, healthy mentoring is indeed bidirectional, with both the mentor and the person being mentored sharing in order to enhance themselves and their relationship; a mentor is not necessarily a "sage on the stage," but rather a "guide on the side" (Smith, 2007). As mentoring is a professional relationship, we will discuss it in greater detail.

> One necessary professional element is a leadership or strategic coach. And if possible, a group of people who can reflect together on what we're learning in order to think strategically. It's hard to create that in an area in which we all know each other because of boundaries, but it's very important.
>
> (Interviewee)

Mentoring: A Special Professional Relationship

As women leaders, some of us have been pioneers—the "first" women to serve in the leadership positions that we hold. Accordingly, the majority of our mentors have been men. In fact, studies show that most women leading at present have a network of men

Don't ask them for the world. Ask them to show you how they did it. Ask them what they would do if they were in your situation. Ask them if you can come talk to them periodically. Over time, they'll buy in. You'll become someone they want to help.

(Interviewee)

to whom they go for career advice (Kolb, Williams, & Frohlinger, 2004). Although almost all of these male-female relationships have ultimately been fruitful for us, we realize that they might not be wholly productive for everyone.

In Western society, male-female mentorships inherently have an added power differential—one that goes beyond the mentor-mentored space—as men are generally seen as more powerful than women. This power differential and its effects have been noted in a variety of sectors; in higher education, for example, single-sex education for women has been found to offer greater academic developmental benefits than co-education. Why? In a single-sex educational environment, students have felt less intimidated to interact with faculty, and this increased interaction has led to more advanced verbal skill development and higher intellectual self-esteem. In a study that focused specifically on mentoring in higher education, women who were mentored noted that they preferred to seek female mentors to avoid developing a father-daughter style relationship with a male mentor (Eliasson, Berggren, & Bondestam, 2000). Free from the added concerns of gender biases, female-female mentoring relationships have often been able to better focus on the personal and professional development of women being mentored. Furthermore, these relationships begin to create an entire network of women who can learn and grow together, stemming feelings of isolation and "otherness" that are common within male-dominated environments (Moultie & de la Rey, 2003).

Networking is valuable in our leadership roles. It helps us demonstrate our capabilities. We don't put ourselves out there. We need to keep asking ourselves: What is my development plan? What do I want to do next and what steps will get me there?

(Interviewee)

In many professions, such as business, academia, and health care, the percentage of women in management positions reaches near parity with that of men; however, women still represent less than one percent of the top leadership positions in the nation (Kolb et al., 2004). Among the many factors that have led to this, it is thought that the tendency for "like to favor like"—in this case, male leaders to support male protégés—has hindered women from attaining the knowledge of, or the opportunity to enter, the informal system of career advancement and has filtered women out of the pipeline to leadership (Scanlon, 1997). Through the information flow that occurs within supportive mentoring relationships and career networks with other women, however, it is hoped that women gain the guidance, affirmation, and tools to break through the glass ceilings and ascend to leadership positions.

MENTORING

During one of our retreats, a participant shared an example of how a mentor can sow the seeds of future success. She spoke about her first position as a manager, which came with numerous budget, property, and personnel headaches. While she was able to navigate through most aspects of managing, she didn't really know how to deal with and understand budgets. Her boss and mentor, the CEO, inspired her through trust. "Take the budget home with you," she said, "and don't get out of your bathrobe until you figure it out! I know you can do this!" Indeed, through this generous gesture, the participant was able to understand budgeting, the benefits of which have lasted a lifetime. She now oversees an organization with over $200M in assets and is always on top of how the finances work.

Of course, challenges can still arise within any mentoring relationship—regardless of the gender pair. The role of power often can become distorted. Mentors and those they mentor sometimes succumb to possessiveness over their work or ideas, which can hinder their development as individuals and as a team (Scanlon, 1997). When working with a "star" mentor, it is easy for a person being mentored to feel that he or she must submit to the mentor or even must become the mentor's personal assistant. For women and other underrepresented people, tokenism, sex-role socialization, or other role-defining traps may also plague mentoring relationships, in which the mentor and person being mentored feel that they must fulfill preconceived, artificial roles that do not allow for them to live out fully their entire identities. In fact, mentoring relationships can become convoluted and even negative when the identity and individuality of the mentor and the person being mentored complicate the relationship and its goals. By taking on a protégé, the mentor acknowledges the promise and the possible new developments that another person can contribute to a field; however, the mentor will not necessarily receive recognition and reward for the protégé's success, even though the mentoring relationship may have been a positive contributing factor. Accordingly, potential mentors may feel that taking on a mentoring relationship will be an acknowledgement of their professional sunset; fearing that they will be bested, they may refuse protégés or develop a toxic relationship with them (Porter-O'Grady & Malloch, 2007). Guidance or formal mentoring programs can help negotiate through this paradox of mentoring to promote the development of healthier relationships.

> *I had a lot of people speaking wonderful things in my life—teachers and mentors.*
>
> (Interviewee)

Inspiring Women Leaders of the Future

Despite these challenges, why do we believe that mentors and role models are important? What exactly do these women and men bring to us? Why do we need them? Why are they valuable? And why do we feel compelled to take the risks and face the challenges to become mentors and role models ourselves?

For many of us, because our lives are so connected, we look to others for examples. Each of us makes our road by walking in some ways—we do not simply copy another—but we gain hope and faith to embark on our own journey from others' examples. We naturally build upon the knowledge and experiences that have come before us. When we see someone who looks like us, has had common experiences, or shares certain qualities with us, it is easier for us to say, "If she can do it, so can I!" Encouragement is invaluable, but sometimes it can take us only so far. As one retreat participant has noted:

> I was in the middle of my master's program at an Ivy League institution before I ever truly believed that I had it in me to aspire to a doctoral program. I grew up in an economically depressed area where few people were academics, and while education was seen as important, my peers and I received little exposure to academia. At one point growing up, I remember suggesting that I become a professor, and my teacher said, "That's a 'publish or perish' world—you don't want to do that!" Although I attended a well-respected college on a full-tuition scholarship and even graduated with a perfect grade-point average, and although my advisor—who was male—commented that I could get a Ph.D., I still never thought of myself as able to do so. It was finally after I read Linda Frost's "Somewhere in Particular," which seemed to describe exactly my experience and tensions with academia that I thought, Wow! I'm not alone, and I can do it!

Women can see their paths ahead—as lawyers, businesswomen—I don't think that women are leaving some of the male-dominated professions because they are failing; they choose to leave because they say, 'Why the hell would I want that? I can make more money and have more time and be in control in my life and not have to deal with a whole lot of BS if I just make my own deal,'—kinda like what I did. And they're doing it . . . Women look at that and say, in part, 'This is a game that I'm not willing to spend what needs to be spent in my life to play. I can get the toys that I want another way. Bye!'

(Interviewee)

Having experienced the joys and challenges of leadership, we want to encourage young women to become leaders. We have overcome hurdles to become the leaders—both for ourselves as well as for the women leaders of the future so that they do not have to start from square one and relearn the lessons that we already learned. It is difficult to speak up for change, to know when it is safe to make mistakes, and to reach out to other kindred spirits for guidance; yet we want to show those who aspire to leadership—through our direct interaction and by example—that it can be done. When we take on the responsibilities of role modeling and mentoring, we must understand and feel secure with our own boundaries, understand that we may make mistakes, and not put ourselves on pedestals. We have to know how we will share our lessons learned and even our failures in ways that will be helpful and healthy with the women we mentor.

There is an intrinsic paradox in looking to women for mentoring, role modeling, and coaching. Seeking guidance, advice, and support from women who have come before implies an openness to follow a path that has already been taken, perpetuating the types of leadership that have been established by a male-dominated culture. Advice about navigating the system assumes that the system will not change too much and that the upcoming woman leader is going to participate in it somehow. This paradox has been noted on the individual level, as well as in studies that reveal a shifting back and forth between people's willingness to be shaped by mentors into a specific role and their desire to control their own paths (Devos, 2004).

Yet, even though our interconnected life will not necessarily permit that we completely avoid preexisting systems, women leaders must be willing to take steps to change the system. The possibility for this resides in looking to women for guidance. Because of their gender, women have not participated in the system in the same way men have; they have had to do things differently. Some may align more with the system than others—and some may have actually forged a divergent path altogether to carve out the career they want and define the values upon which they want to build; but overall, women leaders offer an example of the possibility of change.

Cross-Trainings for the Soul

READINGS

- Jean Lipman-Blumen's (1996) *Connective Leadership: Managing in a Changing World* explains connective leadership through interesting visuals and charts. She divides a nine-pointed star into three sections: direct, relational, and instrumental. If you are more visual in your learning style, this may appeal to you.
- Ken Wilbur's (2001) *A Brief History of Everything* offers interesting insights on culture, society, gender, and spirituality, along with helpful exercises and questions for reflection.
- *To Know as We Are Known: Education as a Spiritual Journey* by Parker Palmer (1993) is a spiritual resource for addressing leadership challenges.
- Susan R. Madsen's (2008) *On Becoming a Woman Leader: Learning from the Experiences of University Presidents* offers an in-depth perspective on the formative experiences and influences of ten female university presidents, as well as lessons for aspiring leaders.

REFLECTIONS

- Think of a person in your life who has impacted you but whom you have never formally thanked. What role did that person play for you? What attitudes, behaviors, and circumstances made this person meaningful to you? Dedicate some of your reflection time to fully appreciating this special person. This can be done through reflection and meditation, or you may take a cue from Seligman (2003) and write a gratitude letter to that person, identifying the specific reasons you are grateful. Then, visit the person and read the letter aloud.
- Consider the gifts and lessons you possess and can share with others. How might you use them to enrich someone else's life? How did you come to recognize your gifts? How can you help another dis-cover and then appreciate her or his gifts?

RHYTHMS & RITUALS

- The book *Wisdom Walk: Nine Practices for Creating Peace and Balance from the World's Spiritual Traditions* by Sage Bennet (2007) offers readers nine avenues grounded in our world's spiritual traditions for spiritual development.
- Clarissa Pinkola-Estés's (1996) book *Women Who Run with the Wolves: Myths and Stories of the Wild Woman Archetype* offers opportunities for book groups to discuss individual stories from this gathering of ancient woman wisdom. These stories often address some of the paradoxes facing women leaders.

CHAPTER TEN

A Habitat for Sustainability— Coming Home

To be rooted is perhaps the most important and least recognized need of the human soul.

—Attributed to Simone Weil

Throughout this book, we have explored many ways to transform the energies in and around us into sustainability, and we have reiterated the critical need to do so now if we want to contribute most fully to the development of a thriving planet. For some, this work may be grand, affecting communities, cultures, and countries. For others, it might be done on a smaller scale with a focus on teams and organizations or families and neighborhoods. Yet in order to do this work, we, too, must thrive. To do so we must make protecting our personal habitats the priority in our lives. We need to ensure that regardless of what is happening around us, no matter how bad a day we are having—and we all will have bad days—we have a consistent space where we can reconnect with our own positive energies so we may continue to share them with the world.

Creating a habitat is about finding *home*—that place where we are most grounded, where we can return spiritually, emotionally, if not physically, to restore, refresh, and reenergize. It is the grown-up equivalent of a child's favorite blanket or a cat's favorite spot on the sofa. When we are connected with that home space, our habitat, we feel safe and able to deal with whatever obstacles present themselves in our paths. We can count on this space, again and again. As long as we know it is available and we can access it, even for a moment, we are stronger.

BREAD PUDDING

I envisioned our retreats as taking place in a safe space—a space in which we could care for ourselves and our fellow participants, where we could deeply feel our connection with Earth, and where we could nurture the psychic and emotional connections among us all. We held many of our initial retreats at the home of one of our retreat participants, who graciously opened up this space for us. In addition to enjoying the beauty of our surroundings and engaging in our retreat exercises, we savored time together around good food.

One of my fondest memories of the retreats was sharing our first dinner together. Upon entering the dining room, I was startled to see a huge tin of hot bread pudding. Bread pudding happens to be one of my all-time favorite desserts, not only because of its taste but because of its place in my childhood.

Born in Harlem, I grew up across the George Washington Bridge in Englewood, New Jersey. After my maternal Grandma passed, it became a Friday evening tradition for my Grandpa, who was a hotel elevator operator in New York City, to come to our house to make bread pudding and spend time with the family. I remember how he would come in, announcing himself in his booming West Indian voice, bringing day-old challah bread. He would then go into the kitchen, where my Mom had already begun to assemble the ingredients, and he would tell us stories while he made the bread pudding.

I loved that hot, right-out-of-the-oven bread pudding! But beyond this, for my family and me, I knew that the bread pudding represented Grandpa's way of telling us that he loved us. And to this day, it has remained our way of keeping him with us in our family and in our memories.

So, at our first retreat, which actually took place in South Carolina—another connection to my past as the birthplace of that same Grandma—I was immediately overwhelmed and ecstatic from my head to my heart to see that we would enjoy bread pudding for dessert. In fact, I was at a loss for words and unconsciously reduced to moans, as I felt more loved and closer to my family with every bite.

Without my background as the context, my enthusiastic reaction to the bread pudding might have seemed a little extreme to the other retreat participants, but it soon became a sensory symbol of the warmth of home and habitat for all of us. Although not everyone can personally say that "home" is a safe holding place, we all nonetheless need a sacred and safe place to be. For me, every bite of the bread pudding brought me closer to a safer space within myself and, paradoxically, closer to a safer space with everyone else in the room.

The opportunity to take part in the *Sustaining Our Spirits* initiative was, in its own way for each of us, an opportunity to find and deepen our connections to the habitat that enriches us. The rich, intense, and sometimes painful conversations that took place during each meeting and over the course of several years allowed each of us as participants to reinforce—and in some cases recover—the radiant, positive energy and sense of peace that we needed for ourselves and that would help us be better leaders.

The group setting proved important for us, as it has for many others. In writing about their journeys as women in academia through spiritual metaphors, Collay, Gehrig, Lesniak, and Mayer (2002) propose that relationship and destiny contribute to the process of maturity that women undergo, both spiritually and intellectually; indeed, these components help women create and sustain environments and perspectives that help them make sense of their experiences as women. The *Sustaining Our Spirits* collective provided just such an opportunity for us and coincides with the prevalence of similar soul-centered groups and the desire for them.

The Wellspring Community for Women in Educational Leadership, a group of women leaders who meet four times a year to discuss their needs and goals and to find support as leaders, is another example of ways women find their grounding with each other (Hackney & Runnestrand, 2003). The Wellspring Community is founded on the belief that "effective, democratic, value-based leadership must begin with a personal and professional formative process . . . , that self-exploration and development are vital to a woman's leading, and that this exploration and development happens more readily when they are involved in self-study and professional inquiry among like-minded others." WoLF (Women's Leadership Forum) is an initiative to develop leadership in women created by Julie Gilbert of Best Buy; it is built around the components of commitment, network, and giving back. It has fostered connection among women within her business and beyond to other communities.

Several of the women we interviewed as part of the *Sustaining Our Spirits* project also drew sustenance from gatherings of like-minded women. In a number of cases, these events were less intentional in the focus on self-discovery and reengagement with participants' spiritual sides than *Sustaining Our Spirits,* Wellspring, or WoLF. Yet they still offered the possibility of talking, laughing, and crying in the company of supportive partners or sisters. Even though these experiences were planned as one-time social or bonding events, they often developed into regular rituals. Women who lived in the same city might meet for breakfast or dinner once a month. Sometimes the get-togethers involved traveling to exotic locations. Regardless of their formality or frequency, the women leaders who participated in these gatherings identified these opportunities to relax and grow with "circles of friends" as incredibly sustaining forces in their lives.

> *I am fortunate God chose to give me this gift. It is my responsibility to use it well and help others see and use their gifts.*
>
> **(Interviewee)**

As we began writing this book, we realized we needed to delve deeper into the process of our retreats to understand what made them so powerful in our lives. We were fortunate to have the voices of the women we interviewed to heighten our understanding. We came to realize that having a close group of colleagues, family, and friends with whom to commune and centered on truth telling is an influential and grounding aspect in our lives. As one of our interviewees noted, "The workplace is not geared to tell you the truth. It's about politically correct, spin, the company line. If I don't have a place for the truth, I miss it." Truth telling in a safe and nurturing environment is as healing as it is freeing. As we shed our accumulated masks and sanitized versions of our truths, our souls are prepared for greater growth and possibility.

We have repeatedly learned that many women yearn for a form of communal sharing. As we recount our experiences and the positive impact on our leadership from gathering in circles of conversation with female colleagues and friends, a frequent response is, "Oh, I wish I could be part of a group like that; that's what I need."

The circle as a forum for promoting equality and sharing is fundamental in many cultural traditions. Dynamic engagement in and with community is part of sustainability. Once they are harnessed, the energy, passion, and desires for sustainability must be shared and passed on.

Global initiatives, like the Millionth Circle that calls people together for positive societal transformation, provide compelling examples. In her book, *Urgent Message from Mother: Gather the Women, Save the World,* Jean Shinoda Bolen (2005) calls women to circles. She also explains the theory behind the movement, which integrates elements of theoretical biology, epidemiology, and psychology:

> Every species has its own morphic field, through which all members of the species are influenced and in turn affect . . . as the millionth circle movement grows through the formation of new circles, it will draw upon the energy or patterns of similar present and past circles . . . and in turn will contribute to this same field. The more circles there are, the easier it is for still more to form, which increases the momentum as a movement grows, until a critical mass tips the scales and changes the behavior of the species. (p. 139)

It is, for me, something that—I can't see it, I can't touch it, I can't smell it, I can't taste it—I can't hear it, except for the small voice inside of me, usually residing somewhere it feels like in my heart, that tells me or that I need to tap into . . . So, spirituality isn't always about the religious part of it, although that is a part of it for me; it's more about connecting to that higher power, knowing that there is something bigger than me, greater than me, wiser than me, and stronger than me that I can tap into if I believe and that's my faith . . . that strong center is there for whatever reason and in whatever shape—that is sustaining.

(Interviewee)

Circles help foster safety, introduce new perspectives, and show us that we are not alone, but as we learned together, much of the work we need to do has to be done by ourselves. The journey to our soul-place is a like a spiral. At the same time we go deeper to prepare our hearts, we are guided upward and outward with an overwhelming spirit of excitement and possibility. The more we center and balance ourselves, the more we can share ourselves with others. As we sift through our life experiences, conjoining our past, present, and future, to reach a point of increasing enlightenment, clarification, and transformation within the self, we are rewarded and led home. It is no wonder that Maslow's hierarchy of needs includes, as part of its very foundation, the existence or security of shelter, of home (Maslow, 1943).

Regardless of whether the initial thought of home conjures feelings of warmth and security or chaos and danger, the need to create a place where you can be and do and that you can call your own is what we mean by creating an essential habitat. When we are connected with it, we have a sustainable, unending power source that we can use for healing. We are at our best when we have defined that particular place or space we can call "home"—and then lead from it!

Cross-Trainings for the Soul

READINGS

▦ The monthly newsletter, *Women in Higher Education,* founded and edited by Mary Dee Wenniger, tells the backstories of many of the happenings in the world of academia, but its greatest value is in its many articles on women in positions of leadership. Treat yourself to a subscription by calling 608-251-3232 or e-mailing women@wihe.com.

▦ The wisdom within J. R. O'Neil's (2000) *Paradox of Success: When Winning at Work Means Losing at Life* is helpful for those who find that sometimes what is called "winning" feels a lot like "losing"!

▦ Check out a spiritual classic by a master in both Eastern and Western religions, *Sadhana, a Way to God: Christian Exercises in Eastern Form.* The author, Anthony de Mello (1978), has several books that have been sources of great comfort to many over the years. His is a unique blend of both mystic traditions.

▦ *It's a Meaningful Life: It Just Takes Practice* is written by Bo Lozoff (2000), a Zen master who has a community of practice in the United States. It is not only a wonderful read with practical everyday advice about how to manage ourselves in a very hectic society, but it also lists a number of Web sites to contact for more information.

▦ *A Path with Heart: A Guide through the Perils and Promises of Spiritual Life* is another classic book from a Zen master, Jack Kornfield (1993). His writings provide both hope and humor in the search to become a more spiritual, reflective person. The meditation can also be found on CD through Sound True at http://www.soundtrue.com.

REFLECTIONS

▦ In *Lost in the Land of Oz: Befriending Your Inner Orphan and Heading for Home,* author Madonna Kolbenschlag (1988) takes the familiar Wizard of Oz story that is embedded in the American culture and brings out the deeper meaning of and also describes "evolutionary" leadership in terms that are challenging and enlightening. This book is a real treasure and offers much material for reflection. In particular, consider the quote from Susan Griffen on the dedication page:

> The earth is my sister; I love her daily grace, her silent daring and how loved I am—how we admire this strength in each other, all that we have lost, all that we have suffered, all that we know we are stunned by this beauty, and I do not forget: what she is to me, what I am to her.

▦ Henry Emmons's (2006) book, *Chemistry of Joy: A Three-Step Program for Overcoming Depression Through Western Science and Eastern Wisdom,* is an incredible resource for sustainability. It offers supports for us as women and leaders, as well as strategies for conducting a soul dialogue, building a house of belonging, creating a circle of trust, and tending your inner garden.

RHYTHMS & RITUALS

▦ Use aromatherapy to create a field of energy in your home or office. This is not perfume, but a fragrance that will help you to keep focused and alert or relaxed and quiet, depending on what you need at the moment. Try several to see which is best for you. Find a fragrance that helps you in the way you need it—to soothe, relax, or energize. Place it in your environment and be comforted by it during difficult times. Even if we are not conscious of aromas, they can make an impact on us emotionally. Aromas can be released with candles (some do not even need to be lit); you can inhale the aromas from small vials that you can keep with you during the day; or you can have a trivet filled with that fragrance on which you place your hot beverage that will then fill your space with aromas.

■ In your "space" at home or at the office, create an altar of objects that are important to you. These could include a picture, a souvenir that reminds you of a special time, or any object (stones, for example) that reminds you of the gifts you have received and those you have to give. Create altars that contain special objects and pictures that help you pray, meditate, or reflect on other aspects of reality and open up other avenues of your spirit. Also, create special memorials at certain times of the year; for example, in November, the Mexican culture celebrates the Day of the Dead or *Dias de los Muertos* and creates *ofrendas* (altars) that memorialize those who have died during the past year. Find your own way to remember others in a special way.

Epilogue: From Evolutionary to Revolutionary Leadership—Leading Into the Future

When our circle for *Sustaining Our Spirits* initially came together, some of us were good friends, and some of us were strangers. We willingly formed a community of support and challenge to hasten our commitment to becoming better and healthier women leaders. The more immediate outcome, long anticipated as a book, became several outcomes, all positive and all enhancing the way women leaders can sustain each another and challenge themselves to grow. Certainly, our story was not free from conflict or differences of opinion, but our differences led each of us to create the leadership role that fit us and our organization.

In this book, we sought to capture the heads and hearts, the souls, of the women who gifted us through their sharing of thoughts and feelings and joined them with our own experiences and perspectives around three questions: What sustains us as leaders? What threatens or challenges our sustainability? What wisdom do we want to pass on to the women coming after us? From our initial retreats as nine through our last three years as five women leaders, we have learned much—and often. We have discovered and reclaimed the role of spirituality as the essence, the life force of healthy, joy-filled, and contributing women leaders. We learned that if we have the courage to open ourselves to the gifts of spirit, we not only are able to contribute to the present, but we are also better able to embrace the unknown future. We become, in the words of Madonna Kolbenschlag (1988), "evolutionary leaders":

> . . . catalysts and people skilled in facilitating feedback, structuring new learning and imagining alternatives . . . leadership that has openness to innovation and sensitivity to creative processes in subsystems . . . We become enhancers of the process within and around ourselves, knowing that our purpose and meaning does not wait for us at the

end of our path to the future, [like] in a Land of Oz, but is immanent in the process itself. (p. 170)

As evolutionary leaders, we, like Earth, continue to innovate and create, using our imagination and being sensitive to the paradoxes of life (Kolbenschlag, 1998).

Within this wisdom, we find the charge for us to move even further ahead; we must now become revolutionary leaders. To do so, we must finally acknowledge and reclaim our relationship with the concept and process of power. Power, originating from the Old French word of *poeir,* means "to be able." Through this definition, we understand power as a given, inherent to us all, rising out of our core beings. By readily embracing and purposefully engaging with power, we use our authentic ability to influence the world in a respectful, healthy, natural way. We should not be surprised to learn that this active engagement with power has long been a defining characteristic of leaders. In the Cherokee Native American community, the highest honor one could receive is the title of "the Ghigau" or "Beloved Woman," which is only conferred on women who have proven their leadership by fighting for the survival of their community (Portman & Garrett, 2005, p. 285).

When we have the courage to harness our power and use it for ourselves and our organizations to impact our communities and our world in ways that are raising the quality of life for all, only then are we truly revolutionary leaders.

Aligned with the wisdom of our planet, revolutionary leadership flows from the Earthview, ending dualistic thinking and bringing together all aspects of our work. Rather than doing things for others, we do things with others and we empower our colleagues and clients to do things for themselves. We recognize that self-determination becomes a form of enhancement for everyone.

We must spend time and care coming to truly know ourselves, yet we must not get stopped by our own shadows or even the light of others. We must bravely lead through inclusive, transparent, and authentic dialogue with others, using our Earthview eyes and voices. And all the while, we must remember that both the ways that we are the same as well as our (visible and invisible) differences are multifaceted and must be honored.

Reentry into daily life after an extraordinary retreat experience, or even after reading a book like this, can feel jarring and disillusioning. It can be challenging to reconcile the insights we gain with the events that take place in our everyday world. It is important to acknowledge this and attempt to make the reentry process as gentle as possible. Setting meaningful, yet realistic, goals can provide a pathway for reentry without overwhelming ourselves and everyone around us. Leaving open time for engaging in dialogue with loved ones—both about our experiences and about the events that have taken place in their lives—upon return can help us adjust and maintain the spiritual energy and sense of renewal we have gained.

Women working together can be great supports for each other—they can become lifelong friends, but that was not the purpose of our work through our retreats or even this book. The greater purpose was to explore the lives of women in leadership, spanning multiple sectors, in order to pass on our learnings. We sought to demonstrate that women leaders can come together, teach, learn, and courageously move forward, knowing that they really are never alone. Our stories have not ended—no, indeed, they are just beginning—as we continue to learn from and with our ever-widening circle of women, together, sustaining our spirits. As Gloria Ladson-Billings (2000) reminds us, as researchers, we must make a deliberate choice between epistemologies that support hegemony or those supporting liberation. Accordingly, it remains the intention of our circle, now broadened by your joining, to acknowledge, yet reach beyond our individualism to actively honor the collective experiences of women leaders, thus laying the foundation for creating counter-hegemonic social constructions of authentically healthy workplaces.

Honoring these lessons propels us to speak for ourselves, for all of our fellow human beings, and for the integrity of the Earth. Walking this path requires us to push past our fears and lead through the power of spirit. Living life fully as women leaders is our right and our responsibility to ourselves and all those in our lives. This is the call to which we must respond. For as the poetess Audre Lorde has said, "When I dare to be powerful—to use my strength in the service of my vision, then it becomes less and less important whether I am afraid." May the energy from our ever-widening circle sustain your spirits, today and tomorrow.

Acknowledgments—Thank You!

Our most sincere thanks to all of the women whose voices have joined ours through interviews and retreats; we remain forever gifted by your sharing of your stories and your time: Alison Chase Radcliffe, artist and musician; Amy Serrano, director/writer/cinematographer; Amy Wohl, President, Wohl Associates; Angela R. Hubbard, Chief Operating Officer, United Way of the National Capital Area; Anonymous, deputy chancellor of a major metropolitan school district; Astrid Chirinos, President, Diverso Global Strategies, Multicultural Marketing and Multicultural Workforce Development Consulting Co.; Bernadeia Johnson, Chief Academic Officer, Minneapolis Public Schools; Carla J. Grantham, LCDR, USCG, RET., currently the Director of Recruiting and Corporate Communications, Analytic Services, Inc.; Cassandra McKinney, Senior Vice President, Retail Products & Sales Management, Comerica Bank; Claudia Chiesi, Ph.D., President of Legacy Alliance Associates, and Producer, Siren Studios; Rev. Dagmar Braun Celeste, Roman Catholic priest, Executive Director of the TYRIAN Network; Demie Kurz, sociologist and Co-Director of Women's Studies, University of Pennsylvania; Denise DeVaan, President/CEO, DeVaan & Associates, Inc.; Diana M. Gurieva, Executive Vice President and CEO, Dyson Foundation; Diane Quattrone-Carroll, MSW, private practitioner; Donna A. Fletcher, Senior Analyst, U.S. Environmental Protection Agency; Dr. Doris A. Taylor, Director, Center for Cardiovascular Repair, University of Minnesota, and pioneer in the field of cardiovascular cell therapy; Eleanor Ellis, musician; Estela Ogiste, M.D., Ph.D., Director of Ophthalmology, North General Hospital, New York; Felicia Hall Allen, President, Felicia Hall Allen & Associates, and attorney, motivational speaker, trainer, consultant, and executive coach; Gaye Todd Adegbalola, blues woman, founding member of Saffire–The Uppity Blues Women, Alligator recording artist, and former Virginia state Teacher of the Year; Gracie P. Coleman, Senior Vice President, Human Resources; Jackie Merritt, artist/musician and songwriter, member of M.S.G.–The Acoustic Blues Trio, Blues Xchange, and retired visual information specialist from NAVFAC Atlantic, Engineering/Architectural Branch, Norfolk, VA, Adjunct Art Instructor (drawing), Thomas Nelson Community College, Hampton, VA, and part-time freelance graphic designer; Jean Green Dorsey, technology consultant, social activist, and innovator; Julie Gilbert, Senior Vice President, Winning with Women powered by

WoLF, retail training and leadership development and employee innovation "The Loop," Best Buy Company; Julie Paris Littell, Chief Operating Officer, Peace-Evolutions, LLC; Lakeesha Ransom, Ph.D., international strategy/international development; Linda Craig, Director, Pesticide Action Network, UK; Martha E. Stark, Commissioner, City of New York Department of Finance; Mary E. McClymont, Vice President, Peace and Social Justice Program, The Ford Foundation; Mary Jo Kreitzer, Director, Center for Spirituality & Healing, Academic Health Center, and Professor, School of Nursing, University of Minnesota; Melody J. Stewart, Judge, Ohio Court of Appeals, Eighth Appellate District; Monica Little, CEO, Little & Company; Peggy Blumenthal, Institute of International Education; Penny A. Ralston, Ph.D., Professor and Dean Emeritus, College of Human Sciences, Florida State University; Resa Lynne Gibbs, physical therapist (22 years of loving service; special interest in stroke [CVA], spinal cord injury [SCI], and amputee rehabilitation), and vocalist/musician (percussionist, kazoo player); Rose Bator, President Emeritus, Common Ground, The Cindy Nord Center for Renewal, Oberlin, Ohio; Suzanne Moe, artist/owner, SuMoe Productions; Theresa Wise, Senior Vice President and Chief Information Officer, Northwest Airlines; Yvonne Abner, IBM.

Appendix

Song Lyrics

"Come to Me in Prayer"
Written and composed by Jackie Merritt, performed by M.S.G.–The Acoustic Blues
Trio. To hear the entire CD, please log on to www.acousticbluesmsg.com.
9/30/03

When your heart is burdened and you have no where to go
Come to Me in Prayer
When your mind is troubled and you feel so all alone
Come to Me in Prayer

Bridge:
Come to Me, come to Me
I will set your soul free
Come to Me, come to Me in Prayer
Salvation is my promise, when you get down on your knees
Come to Me in Prayer

Life has no meaning, if there's nothing you believe
Come to Me in Prayer
My love is your blessing when you're comforted by Me
Come to Me in Prayer

Bridge:
Come to Me, come to Me
I will set your soul free
Come to Me, come to Me in Prayer
Salvation is my promise, when you get down on your knees
Come to Me in Prayer

"If I Were Brave"
Written and performed by Jana Stanfield. For additional information concerning Jana and her music, log on to www.janastanfield.com.

If I were brave, I'd walk the razor's edge
where fools and dreamers dare to tread
and never lose faith even when losing my way
What step would I take today if I were brave?

Sustaining Our Spirits
Works Cited

Andrews, T. (2006). *Animal speak: The spiritual and magical powers of creatures great and small.* St. Paul, MN: Llewellyn Publications.

Arrien, A. (1993). *The four-fold way: Walking the paths of warrior, teacher, healer, and visionary.* New York: Harper Collins.

Aserappa, C. (1999). *The Japanese garden.* San Francisco: Council Oak Books.

Ausberger, D. (1992). *Conflict mediation across cultures: Pathways and patterns.* Louisville: Westminster/John Knox Press.

Bailey, D. (1997). Proceedings from: *Advanced Leadership Institute for Catholic Charities Directors.* Florida: Franciscan Center.

Bailey, D. (2006). Leading from the spirit. In F. Hesselbein & M. Goldsmith (Eds.), *The leader of the future 2: Visions, strategies, and practices for a new era* (pp. 297–302). San Francisco: Jossey-Bass.

Bailey, D., & Neilsen, E. H. (1987). Life scripts as sources of reward for women executive directors. *Affilia, 2*(4), 46–55.

Bailey, D., & Uhly, K. (2008). Leadership. In T. Mizrahi & L. Davis (Eds.), *Encyclopedia of social work* (20th ed.). New York, NY: Oxford University Press and NASW Press.

Beck, R., & Metrick, S. B. (1990). *The art of ritual: A guide to creating and performing your own rituals for growth and change.* Berkeley, CA: Celestial Arts.

Belenky, M. F., Clinchy, B. M., Goldberger, N. R., & Tarule, J. M. (1986). *Women's ways of knowing.* New York: Basic Books.

Bennet, S. (2007). *Wisdom walk: Nine practices for creating peace and balance from the world's spiritual traditions.* Novato, California: New World Library.

Berry (1999). *The great work: Our way into the future.* New York: Bell Tower.

Block, P. (1993). *Stewardship: Choosing service over self-interest.* San Francisco: Berrett-Koehler.

Block, P. (2003). *The answer to how is yes.* San Francisco: Berrett-Koehler.

Bolen, J. S. (2005). *Urgent message from mother: Gather the women, save the world.* Newburyport, MA: Conari Press.

Bolman, L., & Deal, T. (1995). *Leading with soul: An uncommon journey of spirit.* San Francisco: Jossey-Bass.

Boyatzis, R., & McKee, A. (2005). *Resonant leadership: Renewing yourself and connecting with others through mindfulness, hope, and compassion.* Boston, MA: Harvard Business School Press.

Brach, T. (2003). *Radical acceptance.* Boston: Bantam Press.

Cady, D. (2006). Peer conversations shape student spiritual development. *Women in Higher Education, 16*(5), 22–23.

Campbell, J. (1949). *The hero with a thousand faces.* Princeton, NJ: Princeton University Press.

Castaneda, C. (1968). *The teachings of Don Juan: A Yaqui way of knowledge.* New York: Washington Square Press.

Casto, C., Caldwell, C., & Salazar, C. F. (2005). Creating mentoring relationships. Between female faculty and students in counselor education: Guidelines for potential mentees and mentors. *Journal of Counseling and Development, 83*(3), 331–336.

Chan, V., & His Holiness the Dalai Lama. (2004). *The wisdom of forgiveness: Intimate conversations and journeys.* New York: Berkeley Publishing Group.

Chesley, J. (2005). *Overcoming injustice: A tradition of resilience.* Retrieved October 17, 2005, from http://www.advancingwomen.com

Chicago, J. (1979). *The dinner party: A symbol of our heritage.* New York: Anchor Books.

Chodron, P. (1999). *When things fall apart.* Boston: Shambhala.

Chodron, P. (2001). *The places that scare you.* Boston: Shambhala.

Chopra, D. (2004). *The book of secrets: Unlocking the hidden dimensions of your life.* New York: Random House.

Collay, M., Gehrig, S., Lesniak, V., & Mayer, C. (2002). Reimagining our academic journeys through spiritual metaphor. *Advancing Women in Leadership Journal, 10*(1), 1–23.

Collins, J. (2001). *Good to great.* New York: HarperBusiness.

Collins, J. (2005). *Good to great and the social sectors: A monograph to accompany good to great.* New York: Harper Collins.

Colwill, N. L. (1995). Sex differences. In Vinnicombe, S. & Colwill, N. L. (Eds.), *The Essence of Women in Management* (p. 20–34). New York: Prentice Hall.

Csikszentmihalyi, M. (1997). *Finding flow: The psychology of engagement with everyday life.* New York: Basic Books.

Daly, M. (1985). *Beyond God the father.* Boston: Beacon Press.

Dass, R. (1971). *Be here now.* San Cristobal, New Mexico: Lama Foundation.

Delbecq, A. (1999). Christian spirituality and contemporary business leadership. *Journal of Organizational Change Management, 12,* 345–349.

de Mello, A. (1978). *Sadhana, a way to God: Christian exercises in Eastern form.* New York: Bantam Doubleday Dell.

Detrude, J., & Stanfield, V. (2000). Successful women leaders: Achieving resiliency through rituals and resources. *Advancing Women in Leadership Journal, 3*(1), 1–8. Retrieved from http://www.advancingwomen.com/awl/winter2000/detrude-stanfield.html

Devos, A. (2004). The project of self, the project of others: mentoring, women and the fashioning of the academic subject. *Studies in Continuing Education, 26*(1), 67–81.

Dilenschneider, R. L. (2007). *Power and influence: The rules have changed.* New York: McGraw-Hill.

Dreher, D. (1990). *The Tao of inner peace.* New York: Harper Collins.

Drucker, P. (1966). *The Effective Executive.* New York: Harper Collins.

Drucker, P. (1973). *Management: Tasks, responsibilities, practices.* New York: Harper Collins.

Drucker, P. (1992). *Managing the non-profit organization: Principles and practices.* New York: Harper Business.

Eadie, D. C. (1998). Planning and managing strategically. In Edwards, R. L., Yahkey, J. A., & Altpeter, M. A. (Eds.), *Skills for effective management of nonprofit organizations.* (pp. 453–468). Washington, D.C.: NASW Press.

Eisler, R. (1990). *The chalice and the blade: Our history, our future.* New York: Harper Collins.

Eisler, R., & Loye, D. (1998). *The partnership way: New tools for living and learning (2nd ed.).* Brandon, VT: Holistic Education Press.

Eliasson, M., Berggren, H., & Bondestam, F. (2000). Mentor programmes—a shortcut for women's academic careers? *Higher Education in Europe, 25*(2), 173–180.

Emmons, H. (2006). *The chemistry of joy: A three-step program for overcoming depression through Western science and Eastern wisdom.* New York: Fireside.

Firestone, T. (1999). *With roots in heaven: One woman's passionate journey into the heart of her faith.* New York: Penguin.

Follett, M. P. (1924). *Creative experience.* New York: Longman Green and Co.

Fontana. D. (2005). *Meditating with mandalas: 52 new mandalas to help you grow in peace and awareness.* London: Duncan Baird Publishers.

Freire, P. (1981). *Pedagogy of the oppressed.* New York: Continuum.

Friedman, T. L. (2005). *The world is flat: A brief history of the twenty-first century.* New York: Farrar, Straus & Giroux.

Fris, J., & Lazaridou, A. (2006). An additional way of thinking about organizational life and leadership: The quantum perspective. *Canadian Journal of Educational Administration and Policy, 48,* 1–26.

Frost, P. J. (2003). *Toxic emotions at work: How compassionate managers handle pain and conflict.* Boston: Harvard Business School Press.

Frost, L. (1999). "Somewhere in particular": Generations, feminism, class conflict, and the terms of academic success. In D. Looser & E. A. Kaplan (Eds.), *Generations: Academic feminists in dialogue.* Minneapolis: University of Minnesota Press.

Funk, C. (2004). *Outstanding female superintendents: Profiles in leadership.* Retrieved October 17, 2005, from http://www.advancingwomen.com

Gardella, L. G., & Haynes, K. S. (2004). *A dream and a plan: A woman's path to leadership in human services.* Washington, DC: NASW Press.

Gardner, H. (2006). *Five minds for the future.* Boston, MA: Harvard Business School Press.

Goleman, D. (2003). *Destructive emotions: How can we overcome them?: A scientific collaboration with the Dalai Lama.* New York: Bantam Dell.

Greenleaf, R. (1977). *Servant leadership: A journey into the nature of legitimate power and greatness.* Mahwah, NJ: Paulist Press.

Grogan, M. (2002). Laying groundwork for a reconception of the superintendency from feminist postmodern perspectives. *Educational Administration Quarterly, 36*(1), 117–142.

Guba, E. G. & Lincoln, Y. S. (1994). Competing paradigms in qualitative research. In N. K. Denzin and Y. S. Lincoln (Eds), *Handbook of Qualitative Research,* pp. 105–117. Thousand Oaks, CA: Sage Publications.

Hackney, C. E., & Runnestrand, D. (2003). *Struggling for authentic human synergy and a robust democratic culture: The Wellspring Community for Women in Educational Leadership.* Retrieved October 17, 2005, from http://www.advancingwomen.com

Handy, C. (1998). *The hungry spirit.* New York: Broadway Books.

Handy, T. (1994). *The age of paradox.* Boston: Harvard Business School Press.

Hanh, T. N. (1992). *Peace is every step: The path of mindfulness in everyday life.* New York: Bantam Books.

Hanh, T. N. (2004). *Anger: Wisdom for cooling the flames.* New York: Penguin Books.

Harris, C. M., Smith, P. L., & Hale, R. P. (2002). *Making it work: Women's ways of leading.* Retrieved October 17, 2005, from http://www.advancingwomen.com

Heider, J. (1985). *The Tao of leadership: Leadership strategies for a new age.* Boston: Bantam Books.

Heifetz, R. A. (1994). *Leadership without easy answers.* Cambridge, MA: Belknap Press.

Heifetz, R. A., & Linsky, M. (2002). *Leadership on the line: Staying alive through the dangers of leading.* Boston: Harvard Business School.

Hesselbein, F. (2002). *Hesselbein on leadership.* San Francisco: Jossey-Bass.

Houston, J. (1982). *The possible human: A course in enhancing your physical, mental, and creative abilities.* New York: Tarcher/Putnam.

Hudson, M. B., & Williamson, R. D. (2002). *Women transitioning into leadership: Gender as both help and hindrance.* Retrieved October 17, 2005, from http://www.advancingwomen.com

Ibn 'Arabi, M. (2006). *A prayer for spiritual elevation and protection.* Oxford: Anqa Publishing.

Intrator, A., & Scribner, M. (2007). *Leading from within.* San Francisco: Jossey-Bass.

Jandeska, K. E., & Kraimer, M. L. (2005). Women's perceptions of organizational culture, work attitudes, and role-modeling behaviors. *Journal of Managerial Issues, 17*(4), 461–478.

Jung, C. G. (1963a). *Memories, dreams, reflections.* New York: Vintage Books.

Jung, C. G. (1963b). *Psychology and rreligion: West and east.* Translated by R. F. C. Hull. New York: Pantheon books.

Kabat-Zinn, J. (1994). *Wherever you go, there you are: Mindfulness meditation in everyday life.* New York: Hyperion.

Ketelle, D. (1997). Compassionate leadership: opening the delicate doors of the heart. *Thrust for Educational Leadership, 26,* 35.

Kolb, D. M., Williams, J., & Frohlinger, C. (2004). *Her place at the table.* San Francisco: Jossey-Bass.

Kolbenschlag, M. (1988). *Lost in the land of Oz: Befriending your inner orphan and heading for home.* San Francisco: Harper & Row.

Kolditz, T. A. (2007). *In extremis leadership: Leading as if your life depended on it.* San Francisco: Jossey-Bass.

Kornfield, J. (1993). *A path with heart: A guide through the perils and promises of spiritual life.* New York: Bantam Books.

Kurtz, E., & Ketcham, K. (2002). *The spirituality of imperfection: Storytelling and the seed for meaning.* New York: Bantam Books.

Kusy, M., & Essex, L. (2007). Recovering from leadership mistakes. *Leader to Leader, 45,* 14–18.

Ladson-Billings, G. (2000). Racialized discourses and ethnic epistemologies. In N. K. Densin & Y. S. Lincoln (Eds.), *Three epistemological stances for qualitative inquiry: Interpretivism, hermeneutics, and social construction* (p. 257–278). Thousand Oaks, CA: Sage Publications.

Lambert, C. (2007, January-February). The science of happiness: Psychology explores humans at their best. *Harvard Magazine.* Retrieved September 14, 2007, from http://www.harvard magazine.com/2007/01/the-science-of-happiness.html

Law, E. (1993). *The world shall dwell with the lamb: A spirituality of leadership in a multicultural community.* St. Louis, MO: Chalice Press.

Lawrence-Lightfoot, S. (1999). *Respect: An exploration.* New York, NY: Perseus Books.

Leider, R. (2004). *The power of purpose: Creating meaning in your life and work.* San Francisco: Berrett-Koehler Publishers, Inc.

Lesser, E. (1999). *The new American spirituality: A seeker's guide.* New York: Random House.

Levoy, G. (1998). *Callings: Finding and following an authentic life.* New York: Three Rivers Books.

Lipman-Blumen, J. (1996). *Connective leadership: Managing in a changing world.* New York: Oxford University Press.

Louv, R. (2005). *Last child in the woods.* Chapel Hill, NC: Algonquin Books of Chapel Hill.

Lozoff, B. (2000). *It's a meaningful life: It just takes practice.* New York: Penguin Putnam.

Maciariello, J. A. (2006). Peter F. Drucker on executive leadership and effectiveness. In F. Hesselbein & M. Goldsmith (Eds.), *The leader of the future 2: Visions, strategies, and practices for a new era* (pp. 3–27). San Francisco: Jossey-Bass.

Madsen, S. R. (2008). *On becoming a woman leader: Learning from the experiences of university presidents.* San Francisco: Jossey-Bass.

Maslow, A. H. (1943). A theory of human motivation. *Psychological Review, 50,* 370–396.

McCleod, M. (2002). Keeping the circle strong. *Tribal College, 13*(4), 10–14.

Michalko, M. (2006). *Thinker toys: A handbook of creative thinking techniques* (2nd ed.). Berkeley, CA: Ten-Speed Press.

Morris, J. (2007). The current leadership crisis and thoughts on solutions. In T. C. Mack (Ed.), *Hopes and visions for the 21st century* (pp. 250–263). Bethesda, MD: World Future Society.

Moultie, A., & de la Rey, C. (2003). South African women leaders in higher education: Professional development needs in a changing context. *McGill Journal of Education, 38,* 407–420.

Murphy, S. A. (2004). Recourse to executive coaching: the mediating role of human resources. *International Journal of Police Science & Management, 7*(3), 175–186.

Myss, C. (1996). *Anatomy of the spirit: The seven stages of power and healing.* New York: Three Rivers Press.

Nagel, E. (2007). The relationship between spirituality, health beliefs, and health behaviors in college students. *Journal of Religion & Health, 46*(1), 141–154.

Nagler, M. (2001). *Is there no other way? The search for a nonviolent future.* Albany, CA: Berkeley Hills Books.

Naparstek, B. (1995). *Staying well with guided imagery.* New York: Grand Central Publishing.

O'Murchu D. (2007). *Transformation of desire: How desire became corrupted and how we can reclaim it.* Maryknoll, NY: Orbis Books.

O'Neil, J. R. (2000). *Paradox of success: When winning at work means losing at life.* New York: Tarcher/Penguin.

Oshry, B. (1999). *Leading systems: Lessons from the power lab.* San Francisco: Berrett-Koehler.

Owen (1999). *The spirit of leadership.* San Francisco: Berrett-Koehler.

Palmer, P. (1993). *To know as we are known: Education as a spiritual journey.* New York: Harper Collins.

Palmer, P. (2004). *A hidden wholeness: The journey toward an undivided life.* San Francisco: Jossey-Bass.

Parker (1990). *The active life: A spirituality of work, creativity, and caring.* San Francisco: Harper & Row.

Phillips, D. B., & van Ummersen, C. (2003). *The widening gyre: Lessons from the fourth Women Presidents' Summit: Living the present, shaping the future.* Washington, DC: Office of Women in Higher Education, American Council on Education.

Pink, D. H. (2005). *A whole new mind: Why right-brains will rule the future.* New York: Riverhead Books.

Pinkola Estés, C. (1996). *Women who run with the wolves: Myths and stories of the wild woman archetype.* New York: Ballantine Books.

Porter-O'Grady, T., & Malloch, K. (2007). *Quantum leadership* (2nd ed.). Sudbury, MA: Jones & Bartlett.

Portman, T. A. A. & Garrett, M. T. (2005). Beloved women: Nurturing the sacred fire of leadership from an American Indian perspective. *Journal of Counseling & Development, 83,* 284–291.

Rolheiser, R. (1999). *The holy longing.* New York: Doubleday.

Rosener, J. (1990). Ways women lead. *Harvard Business Review, 68,* 119–125.

Rubin, H. (1998). *The princessa: Machiavelli for women.* New York: Dell.

Sapolsky, R. M. (2004). *Why zebras don't get ulcers, 3rd ed.* New York: Henry Holt and Company.

Scanlon, K. C. (1997). Mentoring women administrators: Breaking through the glass ceiling. *Initiatives, 58,* 39–59.

Scharmer, C. O. (2007). *Theory U: Leading from the future as it emerges.* Cambridge, MA: Society for Organizational Learning.

Seligman, M. (2003). *Authentic happiness: Using the new positive psychology to realize your potential for lasting fulfillment.* New York: The Free Press.

Selye, H. (1978). *The stress of life.* New York: McGraw-Hill.

Senge, P. (1990). *The fifth discipline: The art and practice of the learning organization.* New York: Currency/Doubleday.

Senge, P., Kleiner, A., Roberts, C., Ross, R., & Smith, B. (1994). *The fifth discipline fieldbook: Strategies and tools for building a learning organization.* New York: Currency/Doubleday.

Senge, P., Kleiner, A., Roberts, C., Roth, G., Ross, R., & Smith, B. (1999). *The dance of change: The challenges to sustaining momentum in learning organizations.* New York: Currency/Doubleday.

Senge, P., Scharmer, C. O., Jaworski, J., & Flowers, B. S. (2004). *Presence: Human purpose and the field of the future.* Cambridge, MA: Society for Organizational Learning.

Shipka, B. (1997). *Leadership in a challenging world: A sacred journey.* Newton, MA: Butterworth-Heinemann.

Simms, M. (2000). Impressions of leadership through a native woman's eyes. *Urban Education, 35*(5), 637–644.

Smith, B., & Ross, R. (1999). From golf to polo. In P. M. Senge, A. Kleiner, C. Roberts, G. Roth, R. Ross, & B. Smith (Eds.), *The dance of change: The challenges to sustaining momentum in learning organizations* (pp. 108–110). New York: Currency/Doubleday.

Smith, S. (October 2007). *Teaching online: From sage on the stage to guide on the side. Using course development standards to create and evaluate online courses.* Paper presented at the annual program meeting of the Council on Social Work Education, San Francisco.

Sorensen, R. (2005). *History of the paradox: Philosophy and the labyrinths of the mind.* New York: Oxford University Press.

Stark, M. (2003). *Time to treat toxic emotions at work* (Harvard Business School Working Knowledge Archive). Retrieved October 1, 2007, from http://hbswk.hbs.edu/archive/3373.html

Sue, D. W., & Sue, D. (2008). *Counseling the culturally diverse: Theory and practice.* (5th Ed.). San Francisco: Wiley Press.

Swimme, B., & Berry, T. (1992). *The universe story: From the primordial flaring forth to the ecozoic era—a celebration of the unfolding of the cosmos.* New York: Harper Collins.

Taylor, S. E., Klein, L. C., Lewis, B. P., Gruenewald, T. L., Gurung, R. A. R., & Updegraff, J. A. (2000). Biobehavioral responses to stress in females: Tend-and-befriend, not fight-or-flight. *Psychological Review, 107,* 411–429.

Tippett, K. (2007). *Speaking of faith.* New York: Viking Adult.

Vaillant, G. (in press). *Spiritual evolution.* New York: Broadway.

Vinnicombe, S., & Colwill, N. L. (1995). *The essence of women in management.* New York: Prentice Hall.

Wheatley, M. J. (1999). *Leadership and the new science: Discovering order in a chaotic world* (2nd ed.). San Francisco: Berrett-Koehler.

Wheatley, M. J. (2002). *Turning to one another: Simple conversations to restore hope to the future.* San Francisco: Berrett-Koehler.

Wheatley, M. J. (2005). *Finding our way: Leadership for uncertain times.* San Francisco: Berrett-Koehler.

Wheatley, M. J. (2006). *Leadership and the new science: Discovering order in a chaotic world* (3rd ed.). San Francisco: Berrett-Koehler.

Whyte, D. (2002). *Crossing the unknown sea: Work as a pilgrimage of identity.* New York: Riverhead Books.

Wilbur, K. (2007). *A brief history of everything.* Boston: Shambhala.

Sustaining Our Spirits
Bibliography

Barnett, R. (2003). Winning your way. *MPI Leading Women Series, 23*(6), 34–37.

Breathnach, S. B. (1996). *The simple abundance journal of gratitude.* New York: Warner Books.

Carr, J. (2003). A women's support group for Asian international students. *Journal of American College Health, 52*(3), 131–134.

Chesterman, C., Ross-Smith, A., & Peters, M. (2003). Changing the landscape? Women in academic leadership in Australia. *McGill Journal of Education, 38*(3), 421–435.

Clark, M. C., Carafella, R. S., & Ingram, P. B. (1998). Leadership at the glass ceiling: Women's experience of mid-management roles. *Initiatives, 58*(4), 59–70.

Coughlin, L., Wingard, E., & Hollihan, K. (Eds.). (2005). *Enlightened power: How women are transforming the practice of leadership.* San Francisco: Jossey-Bass.

De Casal, C. V., & Mulligan, P. A. (2004). Emerging women leaders' perceptions of leadership. *Catalyst, 33*(2), 25–32.

Gardner, H., & Laskin, E. (1995). *Leading minds: Anatomy of leadership.* New York: Basic Books.

George, B. (2006, October 22). Truly authentic leadership. *US News & World Report, 141*(16), 52–54.

Gerdes, E. P. (2003). *The price of success: Senior academic women's stress and life choices.* Retrieved October 17, 2005, from http://www.advancingwomen.com

Giannini, S. T. (2001). Future agendas for women community college leaders and change agents. *Community College Journal of Research and Practice, 25,* 201–211.

Glazer-Raymo, J. (1999). *Shattering the myths: Women in academe.* Baltimore: Johns Hopkins Press.

Hall, B. (2000). *A Summons to New Orleans.* New York: Simon & Schuster.

Hargreaves, A., & Fink, D. (2003). Sustaining leadership. *Phi Delta Kappan, 84*(9), 693–670.

Harris, M. (1989). *Dance of the spirit: The seven steps of women's spirituality.* New York: Bantam Books.

Harry, L. (1994). *Stressors, beliefs, and coping behaviors of black women entrepreneurs.* New York: Garland Publishing.

Hart, J. Activism among feminist academics: Professionalized activism and activist professionals. Retrieved October 17, 2005, from http://www.advancingwomen.com

Hartman, M. S. (Ed.). (1991). *Talking leadership: Conversations with powerful women.* Piscataway, NJ: Rutgers University Press.

Hutner, F. C. (Ed.). (1994). *Our vision and values: Women shaping the 21st century.* Westport, CT: Praeger.

Kahane, A. (2004). *Solving tough problems: An open way of talking, listening, and creating new realities.* San Francisco: Berrett-Kohler.

Kennedy, D. (2003). Women in leadership. A way of being: reflections, role models, and progress. In D. Kennedy (Ed.), *On a woman's path* [Electronic document]. Louisville, KY: Brown Herron.

Korten, D. (2006). *The great turning: From empire to earth community.* San Francisco: Berrett-Koehler.

Langdon, E. A. (2001). Women's colleges then and now: Access then, equity now. *Peabody Journal of Education, 76*(1), 5–30.

Looser, D., & Kaplan, E. A. (Eds.). (1997). *Generations: Academic feminists in dialogue.* Minneapolis: University of Minnesota Press.

Miller, C. D. & Kraus, M. (2004). Participating but not leading: Women's under-representation in student government leadership positions. *College Student Journal, 38*(3), 423–427.

Mulder, A. E. (2001). Rites of passage: On grand entrances and graceful exits. *Community College Journal of Research and Practice, 25,* 239–241.

Murphy, S. A. (2004). Recourse to executive coaching: The mediating role of human resources. *International Journal of Police Science & Management, 7*(3), 175–186.

Murphy, L. E., & Venet, W. H. (1997). *Midwestern women: Work, community, and leadership at the crossroads.* Bloomington, Indiana: Indiana University Press.

Nidiffer, J., & Bashaw, C. T. (Eds.). (2001). *Women administrators in higher education: Historical and contemporary perspectives.* Albany: State University of New York Press.

Perrault, G. (2005). *Rethinking leadership as friendship.* Retrieved October 17, 2005, from http:// www.advancingwomen.com

Reis, S. M. (2003). Gifted girls, twenty-five years later: Hopes realized and new challenges found. *Roeper Review, 25*(4), 154–157.

Rhode, D. (2003). *The difference "difference" makes: Women and leadership.* Portland, OR: Book News.

Robinson, J. L., & Lipman-Blumen, J. (2003). Leadership behaviors of male and female managers, 1984–2002. *Educational Business. 79*(1), 28–33.

Saltzberg, S. (2002). *Faith: Trusting your own deepest experience.* New York: Riverhead Books.

Serrano, A. (2002). *From society subversives to cultural creatives: The emerging and integral voice of the female artist-activist in the documentation and transformation of a new global society.* Unpublished essay.

Shakeshaft, C. (1987). *Women in educational administration.* Thousand Oaks, CA: Sage Publications.

Skog, S. (1995). *Embracing our essence: Spiritual conversations with prominent women.* Deerfield Beach, Florida: Health Communications, Incorporated.

Spears, L. C. (2002). *The servant-leader: From hero to host. An interview with Margaret Wheatley by Larry C. Spears of the Greenleaf Center for Servant-Leadership and John Nobel, director of the Greenleaf Centre.* Retrieved October 14, 2005, from http://www.margaretwheatley.com/ writing.html

Spretnak, C. (Ed.). (1982). *The politics of women's spirituality.* New York: Anchor Press, Doubleday.

Stout-Stewart, S. (2005). Female community-college presidents: Effective leadership patterns and behaviors. *Community College Journal of Research and Practice, 29,* 303–314.

Sturnick, J. A., Milley, J. E., & Tisinger, C. A. (Eds.). (1991). *Women at the helm: Pathfinding presidents at state colleges & universities.* Washington, DC: American Association of State Colleges and Universities.

Teasdale, W. (1997). The inter-spiritual age: Practical mysticism for the third millennium. *Journal of Ecumenical Studies, 34*(1), 74–91.

Twombley, S. (1998). Women academic leaders in a Latin American university: Reconciling the paradoxes of professional lives. *Higher Education, 35,* 367–397.

Vinnicombe, S., & Colwill, N. L. (1995). *The essence of women in management.* New York: Prentice Hall.

Wheatley, M. J. (1998). Love and fear in organizations. *National Association of Student Personnel Administrators Newsletter, 20*(5). Retrieved October 14, 2005, from http://www.margaret-wheatley.com/writing.html

Wheatley, M. J. (1998). Reclaiming Gaia, reclaiming life. In: *The Fabric of the Future.* Newburyport, MA: Conari Press. Retrieved October 14, 2005, from http://www.margaretwheatley.com/writing.html

Wheatley, M. J. (2002). *Turning to one another: Simple conversations to restore hope to the future.* San Francisco: Berrett-Koehler.

Wheatley, M. J., & Chodron, P. (1999). It starts with uncertainty. *Shambala Sun.* Retrieved October 14, 2005, from http://www.margaretwheatley.com/writing.html

Women—An endangered species. (1987). *World Development Forum, 5*(21), 1–2.

Woods, G. (2007). The "Bigger Feeling": The importance of spiritual experience in educational leadership. *Educational Management Administration & Leadership, 35*(1), 135–155.

Woolf, V. (1929). *A room of one's own.* Retrieved December 12, 2005, from University of Adelaide e-books, http://etext.library.adelaide.edu.au/w/woolf/virginia/w91r/

Index

Abbesses, 91

Agape, 7, 26

Alienation, 44

Alters, 108

Analysis, 18

Anatomy of the Spirit: The Seven Stages of Power and Healing (Myss), 27

Anderson, Marian, 67

Andrews, Ted, 15

Anger: Wisdom for Cooling the Flames (Hanh), 65

Animal Speak, The Spiritual and Magical Powers of Creatures Great and Small (Andrews), 15

Anthony, Susan B., 91

Aromatherapy, 107–108

Arrien, Angeles, 15

Ausberger, David, 93

Authenticity
challenges to, 48–50, 54
explanation of, 24–25
leadership and, 69

Balance
challenges to, 51–52
spirituality and, 82

Belenky, M. F., 62

Benchmarking, 18

Bennet, Sage, 102

Berry, Thomas, 33n, 55, 82

Block, Peter, 77

Bohr, Niels, 32

Bolen, Jean Shinboda, 105–106

Boundaries
function of, 80–81
tensions in, 84

Boyatzis, R., 52, 53

A Brief History of Everything (Wilbur), 102

Budgeting, 19

The Chalice and the Blade: Our History, Our Future (Eisler), 93

The Chemistry of Joy: A Three-Step Program for Overcoming Depression Through Western Science and Eastern Wisdom (Emmons), 86, 107

Chesley, J., 75

Chödrön, Pema, 29, 58

Circles, 105–106

Coaches, 97

Collaboration, 19

Collay, Michelle, 15, 104

Collins, Jim, 58

Colwill, N. L., 62

"Come to Me in Prayer" (Merritt), 115–116

Communication
female leaders and, 62–63
gender and, 62–64
technological advances in, 18

Community
discovery of, 88–89
importance of, 87–88
value of, 7–8, 87

Compassion, 25

Conflict Meditation Across Cultures: Pathways and Patterns (Ausberger), 93

Connective Leadership: Managing in a Changing World (Lipman-Blumen), 102

Convention on the Rights of Women, 91

Courage, 25

Creating, 19

Creativity, 34

Dalai Lama, 31, 33
Daly, Mary, 88
Day of the Dead, 108
Decision making, 19
Delbecq, A., 37
The Devil Wears Prada, 49, 50
Dialogue, 6–8
Dreams, 58
Dreher, Diane, 38
Drucker, Peter, 19, 67

Earth
  connections with, 35, 55, 89
  sustainable development and, 82
  toxicity rebalancing by, 55
  view of, 31–32
Earthview
  cosmological principles of, 33
  explanation of, 29, 31–32
  interconnectivity and, 31–34, 37
  organizational environment and, 83–84
  spirituality and, 36
  Sustaining Our Spirits retreats and, 36
Eisler, Riane, 93
Emmons, Henry, 107
Empathy, 25
Employee appraisals, 20
Employees, 20
Enneagram, 78
Environment, 80
Ereshkigal, 93
Essex, L., 25
Estés, Clarissa Pinkola, 16
Exercise, 86

Faith. *See also* Spirituality
  explanation of, 7
  of leadership, 25–26
  living our missions and, 75–76
Fast Company, 27
Fear
  culture of, 45, 54
  paths to overcoming, 57
Feminist, 92
Follett, Mary Parker, 91
Fontana, David, 77
Food, 93, 104
Forum on Religion and Ecology, 15
The Four-fold Way: Walking the Paths of
    Warrior, Teacher, Healer and Visionary
    (Arrien), 15
Freire, Paulo, 6
Frost, Peter, 42, 46, 58

Gardner, Howard, 8
Gehrig, Sandy, 15, 104

Gender, communication and, 62–64
Gilbert, Julie, 105
Goleman, Daniel, 33
Grim, John, 15
Grimme, John, 82
Guided imagery, 86

Handy, Charles, 68, 70, 71, 76
Hanh, Thich Nhat, 31, 65
Healers, 46–48
Heider, John, 65
Heifetz, R. A., 44, 53, 58, 60
Heroes, 96
Hierarchy of needs (Maslow), 106
Hope, 7
Houston, Jean, 27
Howard, Jean, 87
Humility, 7, 25

Inanna, 93
Interconnectivity, 31–34, 37
Internet, 18
Intrator, Sam M., 58
Invitation Method, 10
It's a Meaningful Life: It Just Takes Practice
    (Lozoff), 107

The Japanese Garden (Aserappa), 87
Journaling
  function of, 15–16, 63
  suggestions for, 65
Jung, Carl, 68, 74

Keller, Helen, 3
Kolbenschlag, Madonna, 107, 109–110
Kornfield, Jack, 107
Kusy, M., 25

Ladson-Billings, Gloria, 110
LaDuke, Winona, 95
Last Child in the Words (Louv), 33
Lawrence-Lightfood, S., 60
Leaders
  addressing shadows, 74–75
  boundary establishment by, 80–81
  challenges to self, 52–54
  encouraging women to be, 100–101
  expectations of, 48, 56
  females of color as, 61
  hierarchical structure of, 49
  loneliness in, 52, 53
  need for connection in, 37, 53
  stereotypes of female, 48
  as toxin handlers, 46–48
  vision and mission of, 67–68

Leadership
    alienation and, 44
    critical competencies for, 18–20
    decision making function of, 19
    exploration of, 12–13
    female approach to, 41–42
    humility and, 7, 25
    mentoring and, 97–99
    metaphor for, 15
    in Native American cultures, 31, 69, 110
    overview of, 17–18
    paradoxes for, 9
    radical self-help and, 84
    revolutionary, 110
    spirituality and, 22–24, 82, 83
    sustaining balance in, 51–52
    Western view of, 29–30
Leadership and the New Science: Discovering Order in a Chaotic World (Wheatley), 38
Leadership on the Line: Staying Alive Through the Dangers of Leading (Heifetz & Linsky), 58
Leadership Without East Answers (Heifetz), 58
Leading from Within (Intrator & Scribner), 58, 65
Leider, Richard, 70
Leonard, Linda Schiese, 16
Lesniak, Valerie, 15, 104
Lesser, E., 60–61
Levoy, Gregg, 68
Linsky, M., 44, 53, 58, 60
Lipman-Blumen, Jean, 102
Loneliness, 52, 53
Lost in the Land of Oz: Befriending Your Inner Orphan and Heading for Home (Kolbenschlag), 107
Louv, Richard, 38
Love, 7, 26
Lozoff, Bo, 107

Maciariello, J. A., 19
Madsen, Susan R., 102
Mandala, 77
Mandala Project, 77
Mankiller, Wilma, 79
Maslow's hierarchy of needs, 106
Mayer, Carol, 15, 104
McCleod, M., 69
McKee, A., 52, 53
Meditating with Mandalas: 52 New Mandalas to Help You Grow in Peace and Awareness (Fontana), 77
Mello, Anthony de, 107
Mentors, 97–99
Merritt, Jackie, 115
Metaphor, 8, 15

Microaggression, 48–49
Millionth Circle, 105
Mind–body–spirit connection, 33, 48
Mission
    faith and, 75–76
    internal and external constellations and, 73–74
    leadership and, 67–68
    living our, 69–73, 75–76
    personal, 68–70
    personal vs. organizational, 73–74
Mobius, August Ferdinand, 79
Mobius strip, 79
Multiculturalism, 49
Music, 27
Myers–Briggs Type Indicator, 78
Myss, Caroline, 27

Naparstek, Belleruth, 86
National Aeronautics and Safety Administration (NASA), 31–32
Native American cultures
    communal relationships in, 90
    nature of leadership in, 31, 69, 110
    relationship with natural world, 31
Needs, Maslow's hierarchy of, 106
Noether, Amalie Emmy, 32

O'Murchu, Diarmuid, 27, 90
On Becoming a Woman Leader: Learning from the Experiences of University Presidents (Madsen), 102
O'Neil, J. R., 107
Organizations
    disconnect in, 17–18
    dissonance in, 42
    effect of technological advances on, 18
    healers in, 46–48
    toxicity in, 42–48, 50, 54–56, 60
Oshry, Barry, 77

Palmer, Parker J., 74, 77, 79, 86, 102
Parabola: Myth, Tradition and the Search for Meaning, 77
Paradox
    function of, 8–9
    management of, 70–73, 75–76
Paradox of Success: When Winning at Work Means Losing at Life (O'Neil), 107
The Partnership Way: New Tools for Living and Learning (Eisler & Loye), 93
A Path with Heart: A Guide through the Perils and Promises of Spiritual Life (Kornfield), 107
Patience, 26

Penkola-Estés, Clarissa, 102
Perera, Sylvia Brinton, 16
Phillips, D. B., 74
Physical exercise, 86
Physics, 32
Pink, Daniel, 8
Power stress, 52–53
The Princessa: Machiavelli for Women (Rubin), 93

Quantum interconnectedness, 32

Radical self-help, 84
Reflections
    function of, 6
    through journaling, 15–16
"Reimagining Our Academic Journeys Through Spiritual Metaphor" (Collay et al.), 15
Religion, 22. *See also* Faith; Spirituality
Resistance, 42
Resource development, 19
Retreats. *See Sustaining Our Spirits* retreats
Rich, Adrienne, 41
Ritual
    in daily lives, 10
    function of, 9–10
    physical exercise as, 86
Role models, 96
Rolheiser, R., 75
Ross, R., 51
Rubin, Harriet, 93
Rumi, Jelaluddin, 65

Sadhana, a Way to God: Christian Exercises in Eastern Form (Mello), 107
Scharmer, C. Otto, 86
Scribner, Megan, 58
Self-help, radical, 84
Self-knowledge
    finding mission through, 68–69
    overview of, 60–61
    tests to aid in, 78
Seligman, M., 102
Senge, Peter, 86
Singer, June, 16
Smith, B., 51
Snowball sampling, 4
Sorensen, R., 19
Soul, 23
Spiritual Evolution (Vaillant), 33
Spirituality. *See also* Faith
    as centeredness, 82
    Earthview and, 36
    elements of, 24–26
    explanation of, 22

leadership and, 22–24, 82, 83
of living our mission, 75–76
overview of, 20–21
principles of global, 75–76
Stanton, Elizabeth Cady, 91
Stereotypes, 48
Storytelling, 90–92
Strategic planning, 20
Stress
    mind–body–spirit connection and, 48
    power, 52–53
Sustainable development, 82
Sustaining Our Spirits retreats
    background of, 4–5, 9, 10–14
    change in location of, 89
    Earthview and, 36
    participants in, 85
    role of nature in, 81
    value of, 110–111
Swimme, Brian, 33, 55, 82
Synchronicities, 68, 71

Taoism, 31, 65, 87
The Tao of Inner Peace (Dreher), 38
The Tao of Leadership: Leadership Strategies for a New Age (Heider), 65
Technological advances, 18, 20
Theory U, 86
Thompson, Dorothy, 59
Time management, 19
Tippett, Krista, 76
To Know as We Are Known: Education as a Spiritual Journey (Palmer), 102
Toxic Emotions at Work: How Compassionate Managers Handle Pain and Conflict (Frost), 42, 58
Toxicity
    explanation of, 42
    fear and, 44–45
    in interpersonal relationships, 51
    lessening impact of, 45–48
    microaggression as, 48–49
    organizational, 42–45, 50, 54–56, 60
Transformation of Desire: How Desire Became Corrupted and How We Can Reclaim It (O'Murchu), 27
Travel, 93
Truth, Sojourner, 91
Tucker, Mary Evelyn, 15, 82

United Nations Commission on Sustainable Development, 82
United Nations Environment Programme, 82
Urgent Message from Mother: Gather the Women, Save the World (Bolen), 105–106

Vaillant, George, 33
van Ummersen, C., 74
Violence, 54
Visioning, 20

Weil, Wimone, 103
Wellspring Community for Women in
    Educational Leadership, 104–105
Wenninger, Mary Dee, 107
Western worldview
    dominance of, 29–30
    explanation of, 30
    organizational structure and, 41
Wheatley, Margaret, 33, 38, 60, 83
Whyte, David, 60
Wilbur, Ken, 102
*Wisdom Walk: Nine Practices for Creating Peace
    and Balance from the World's Spiritual
    Traditions* (Bennet), 102
WoLF, 105
Wollstonecraft, Mary, 91
Women
    of color, 61
    degrading pressures on, 54

leadership approach of, 41–42
leader stereotypes of, 48
microaggression experienced by, 49
multiple roles of, 52
networks of, 89–90
nurturing styles of, 47
sense of community for, 88
sources of guidance for, 95–97
storytelling and, 90–92
as toxin handlers, 46–48
voice for, 62–63
Women in Higher Education, 107
Women's Ways of Knowing (Belenky et al.),
    62
*Women Who Run with the Wolves: Myths and
    Stories of the Wild Woman Archetype*
    (Penkola-Estés), 102
Woodman, Marion, 16
Workplace
    balancing relationships in, 49, 52
    challenges in, 50–51
Worldviews
    Eastern and indigenous, 31
    Western, 29–30, 41